UNDERSTANDING STEWART O'NAN

UNDERSTANDING CONTEMPORARY AMERICAN LITERATURE

Matthew J. Bruccoli, Founding Editor

Linda Wagner-Martin, Series Editor

Also of Interest

Understanding Andre Dubus, by Olivia Carr Edenfield
Understanding August Wilson, by Mary L. Bogumil
Understanding Colson Whitehead, by Derek C. Maus
Understanding James Baldwin, by Marc Dudley
Understanding Jane Smiley, by Neil Nakadate
Understanding John Edgar Wideman, by D. Quentin Miller
Understanding John Updike, by Frederic Svododa
Understanding Jonathan Lethem, by Matthew Luter
Understanding Michael Chabon, by Joseph Dewey
Understanding Randall Kenan, by James A. Crank
Understanding Richard Russo, by Kathleen Drowne
Understanding Ron Rash, by John Lang

UNDERSTANDING STEWART O'NAN

Heike Paul

THE UNIVERSITY OF SOUTH CAROLINA PRESS

Published by the University of South Carolina Press
Columbia, South Carolina 29208

www.uscpress.com

Manufactured in the United States of America

29 28 27 26 25 24 23 22 21 20
10 9 8 7 6 5 4 3 2 1

Library of Congress Cataloging-in-Publication Data
can be found at http://catalog.loc.gov/.

ISBN 978-1-64336-149-9 (hardback)
ISBN 978-1-64336-150-5 (paperback)
ISBN 978-1-64336-151-2 (ebook)

For Klaus,
Niagara Falls, anytime

CONTENTS

SERIES EDITOR'S PREFACE

The Understanding Contemporary American Literature series was founded by the estimable Matthew J. Bruccoli (1931–2008), who envisioned these volumes as guides or companions for students as well as good nonacademic readers, a legacy that will continue as new volumes are developed to fill in gaps among the nearly one hundred series volumes published to date and to embrace a host of new writers only now making their marks on our literature.

As Professor Bruccoli explained in his preface to the volumes he edited, because much influential contemporary literature makes special demands, "the word *understanding* in the titles was chosen deliberately. Many willing readers lack an adequate understanding of how contemporary literature works; that is, of what the author is attempting to express and the means by which it is conveyed." Aimed at fostering this understanding of good literature and good writers, the criticism and analysis in the series provide instruction in how to read certain contemporary writers—explicating their material, language, structures, themes, and perspectives—and facilitate a more profitable experience of the works under discussion.

In the twenty-first century Professor Bruccoli's prescience gives us an avenue to publish expert critiques of significant contemporary American writing. The series continues to map the literary landscape and to provide both instruction and enjoyment. Future volumes will seek to introduce new voices alongside canonized favorites, to chronicle the changing literature of our times, and to remain, as Professor Bruccoli conceived, contemporary in the best sense of the word.

Linda Wagner-Martin, Series Editor

ACKNOWLEDGMENTS

Many years ago, Anne Koenen first introduced me to Stewart O'Nan's writing, and I want to thank her for that. Linda Wagner-Martin has supported this project as part of her Understanding Contemporary American Literature series at the University of South Carolina Press, and I owe her my profound gratitude for her generosity and her patience. This book could have found no better home. At the press, Aurora Bell has been a superb editor. I am also grateful to the two anonymous readers for their helpful advice.

Further, I wish to thank Susen Faulhaber for her admirable diligence in handling the manuscript—proofreading, checking references (and checking them yet again) as well as organizing the bibliography. Alex Sukles has been a fabulous research assistant, Sarah Marak has commented in valuable ways on the manuscript, and Sebastian Schneider has been an excellent reader-editor. My deepest gratitude to Klaus Loesch for his help and support!

Thanks to Anne Stockton who has generously shared her *The Speed Queen*–on stage experiences with me.

Finally, I want to express my gratitude to Stewart O'Nan for kindly agreeing to an interview for this volume (to be found in the appendix) and, of course, for writing such wonderful books.

The labor on this book has been funded by the German Research Foundation (Leibniz funds).

CHAPTER 1

Understanding Stewart O'Nan

Stewart O'Nan has been a highly visible presence on the literary scene ever since his short story collection *In the Walled City* (1993) and his novel *Snow Angels* (1994) were published to great critical acclaim. In 1996, *Granta* literary magazine named O'Nan one of the best young American novelists, and his literary productivity, versatility, and range have impressively confirmed this appraisal and, if anything, steadily enhanced his reputation over the years. To date, his published work includes sixteen novels, several books of nonfiction, a screenplay, and two short story collections (one of them a short story cycle), and his writings have been translated into many languages including French, German, Italian, Spanish, and (Brazilian) Portuguese. In short, he has become a writer of international popularity and acclaim. With an output of almost a book a year, he has been described as "our best working novelist."[1]

While his audience has continuously increased over the decades, scholarship on his work has hardly kept pace at all. In fact, to this day critical work on his fiction consists mostly of reviews, review essays, and interviews. Hence, a critical appraisal of the writer and his work is long overdue. Stewart O'Nan, like few other contemporary American writers, captures the spirit of America in the very moment; he does so with an unflinching gaze at the (at times harsh) realities people face, and he describes their everyday lives with much detail and precision in a mode that recalls the best of classic realist texts. This volume sets out to be the first comprehensive study of Stewart O'Nan's writings. Even if not every single text of O'Nan can be addressed at length in what follows, the chapters in this volume deal with his most significant works to date and identify major themes and representational strategies, as varied and diverse as they might be. Given his broad oeuvre, these readings can only be exemplary rather than exhaustive and should be considered as an invitation for further inquiry.

Paradoxically, one reason for the lack of scholarship on O'Nan's fiction may be the versatility of the author and the multiplicity of his writings. Perhaps more than any other contemporary author, O'Nan seems to be reinventing his role as a writer with each new book, perpetually changing genres and narrative perspectives, twisting formulas, and exploring different settings and topics. His shape-shifting literary idiom—almost every book of his varies in subject, length, and approach—makes it difficult to categorize him as a writer despite his specific style, and his thematic concerns with the seemingly unspectacular of everyday life may be another reason for the relative lack of scholarly interest toward his body of work so far.

Certain developments and core characteristics in his work, however, become discernible in a *longue-durée* perspective. Over the years, his writing has oscillated between fast-paced plot-driven tales with a suspense-oriented aesthetic and novels of manners with a subtler slice-of life aesthetic, but there is an increasing tendency toward the latter. O'Nan at times offers what would conventionally be considered a gripping tale, but in other cases he manages to keep his reader glued to the page with a story lacking in action such as a wife waiting patiently for her husband to be released from prison, or an elderly widow who spends her days not doing much of anything, or the usual routine of a family holiday; in spite of (or maybe because of) the ostensible uneventfulness of the lives he describes, he holds his audience. One of the questions this volume seeks to answer is simply: how does he do that? A tentative answer to this question may be found in his specific neorealist aesthetics that navigates surface and depth in his literary works and that successfully links quotidian matters of American life to instances of the unknown or unknowable, or even the uncanny. The latter resides as much in the world "out there" as in the interiority or—for lack of a better word—the humanity of his characters.

STEWART O'NAN'S writing career is somewhat unusual, to say the least. Born in 1961 in Pittsburgh, Pennsylvania, where he was also raised, O'Nan had a first career as an engineer, as it were, an unhappy engineer, who spent his spare time writing fiction in his basement. After earning his bachelor of science in aerospace engineering from Boston University in 1983, he worked as a test engineer for a company in Bethpage, New York, and was involved with such technology as the Space Shuttle and other military equipment. Following the advice and encouragement of his wife, he eventually quit his job and went back to school: to the prestigious master of fine arts program at Cornell University, from which he graduated in 1992 with a master in fiction writing (the institution today holds his papers in its rare collections). With his first published prose, he catapulted himself onto the literary scene, where he has remained ever since. His

Cornell experience, thus, was a turning point in his life; he has been a professional writer as well as a teacher of creative writing ever since.

As his main literary influences or models, Stewart O'Nan most often names Stephen King, with whom he has collaborated on several projects, and Flannery O'Connor—two very different writers, at first glance, who share a predilection for exploring the supernatural and the uncanny, respectively. In addition, we find references in his interviews to Edgar Allan Poe (about whose life he wrote a screenplay), William Maxwell, and Alice Munro.[2] Different authors seem to have exerted their influence on different texts, and this may have contributed to O'Nan's astonishing flexibility in terms of style and literary inventiveness.

Certainly, O'Nan is knowledgeable and versatile in a great number of different genres. His writings can be characterized as drawing on specific genres, such as the road novel (*The Speed Queen*), the western (*A Prayer for the Dying*), the love story (*The Odds*), the family chronicle (*Wish You Were Here; Emily, Alone; Henry, Himself*), and the Hollywood novel (*West of Sunset*) as well as the gothic tale or the ghost story (*The Night Country*). Rather than simply emulating these genres and using their generic formulas, he plays with, modulates, and expands their specific conventions, at times also crossing them and creating new hybrid novelistic forms. Stewart O'Nan is obviously interested in the mastery of writing as a craft rather than in writing as a means to establish (or fit into) a brand or to cater to a particular niche market. He still refers to his work as a "learning process."[3] Hence, his texts are not drawing attention to a specific style or school or to the author's reputation but instead focus on the characters and their fate—and they do provide what one might call a good read. At the same time, he has remained quite unpredictable as a writer: even as we find recurring themes and concerns, readers are potentially in for a surprise with every new book.

Following from that observation, Stewart O'Nan, like few other contemporary writers, manages to cater both to more academically minded readers who appreciate literary sophistication and intertextuality as well as to a more general audience of popular fiction. Overall, he is not often considered a writer's writer or a literary writer by literary critics (the scholarly archive would be more substantial in that case) but rather as a popular middlebrow author. On several occasions, he has even teamed up with Stephen King to write about sports—about their shared love of the Red Sox and the historic 2004 season in the nonfiction piece *Faithful* and about a man watching baseball games only to see the faces of dead people in the audience in their gothic novella *A Face in the Crowd*. According to Bev Vincent, Stephen King began to spin the latter story at the 2012 Savannah Book Festival and asked his audience to come up with a full-fledged narrative and an ending; Stewart O'Nan, who happened to be in the audience, did just that, and King and O'Nan ended up writing the final story together.[4]

At the same time, Stewart O'Nan is certainly also a postmodern writer due to the ways his works often have a visual or even cinematic quality produced by specific formal elements, such as the prominent use of chapters resembling vignettes or *tableaux vivants.* These vignettes often appear as a long series of scenes the reader is tasked with connecting to each other, not least by filling in narrative gaps in a way that evokes how meaning is generated in film through cutting between scenes. The author, in this instance and others, appropriates specific techniques from other media (photography, performance, film) and turns them into literary devices. It is surprising that so far only one of his novels has been made into a film (*Snow Angels,* with Kate Beckinsale and Sam Rockwell, 2007), as reading one of his books is often an experience similar to watching a film. But as the rights to several of his books have been optioned, we may expect more film adaptations of his works to follow (see the appendix). On the whole, O'Nan's writing draws on strategies of intermediality.

After this more general appraisal or description of Stewart O'Nan's work that situates his writing in the contemporary moment on the American literary scene, several features seem to characterize his literary idiom more distinctly and appear to be the specific hallmarks of his texts. First, the everyday, the ordinary, and "the mundane" loom large in O'Nan's fiction, and he writes with an eye to detail, specificity, and real-life repetitiveness (although not in a boring or redundant way) that at times appears almost journalistic in style.[5] O'Nan's literary universe is not one of epiphanies and pathos but rather one of contingencies, streaks of bad (or good) luck, and everyday pleasures and pains. His slice-of-life aesthetic is deceptively simple and often makes abundant use of dialogue. The role and power of dialogue in his work can be seen in the ways he uses it both to characterize the protagonists and to move the plot forward. Yet behind the descriptions of the quotidian lie uncanny chasms: the "everyday gothic," as I call it, may be Stewart O'Nan's most profound literary invention. While some of his texts actually present straightforward noir tales, even those that do not bear outward signs of the gothic (in the sense of the generic) show moments of the everyday gothic. The everyday gothic is discernible as a transformation of the gothic proper and appears in subtler forms—that is, as slight premonitions, perceived concealed patterns, or echoes of some other truth in representations of everyday life and ordinary settings. Still, it intimates what may be beneath the surface, but it usually does not produce revelations or closure: life simply goes on, dark areas remain in the shadows—and that may at times be the most uncanny thing of all. With Henry James we may identify "those most mysterious of mysteries, the mysteries which are at our own doors" as holding a special place in O'Nan's fiction, through which he has added a new twist to gothic literature in America.[6] In overt and in more subtle ways, therefore, Stewart O'Nan is a writer of gothic fiction.

The so-called American way of life we encounter in Stewart O'Nan's fiction unfolds in minor matters and is often evoked in references to consumer culture and brand names. The "Americanness" of Champale, Snickers, Marlboro, Crest, Zippo lighters, and Ray-Bans needs no explanation and yet orients and anchors the reader in a particular time and place; O'Nan's literary idiom has a way of specifically placing us in the story's national, regional, and more specifically local setting (mostly small-town America). At times, he has been referred to as a regional writer or as a Pittsburgh writer, but his topics clearly go beyond the local color frame. The contemporaneousness of his settings is evoked in the ways his characters are tied to practices of consumption and the marketplace (be it shopping malls, gas stations, motels, or fast food chains), and these are generic, not necessarily regional. The pop-cultural archive encompasses car brands, book titles, song lyrics, and movies. Regarding the prominence of food and the places of its consumption in O'Nan's work, one reviewer has even referred to O'Nan's "junk-food universe," as fast food and restaurant chains appear frequently in his texts from the perspective of both customers and food service workers.[7] Still, the author does not dwell on the cultural iconicity of brands as a pop artist would, nor does he elevate them to the status of universal world-literary props or phenomena. Rather, they are mostly part and parcel of a specific communicative code Stewart O'Nan employs in his neorealist literary style in order to provide orientation, establish familiarity, and allow for identification—plus, in a second step, to make us take another look at what we often deem all too familiar, that is, to slightly defamiliarize it. Hence, as a second major characteristics of his work, exceeding these seemingly banal references to American consumer culture, O'Nan investigates American mythologies, particularly those involving class and social mobility. Among the various labels he has been given is that of "the bard of the working class."[8] Many of his books have small-town middle- or lower-class settings and feature characters who struggle existentially to make ends meet. Notwithstanding his stake in social empathy and (socio)cultural criticism, all of O'Nan's concerns are described in the register of the unsentimental or even antisentimental. His writing thus produces and offers alternative terms of engagement to the kind of false sentimentality that has been identified by scholars such as James Baldwin or Lauren Berlant (*Female Complaint*) as a dominant style in American culture.[9] Rather than engaging in sentimental pathos, O'Nan's tone is often laconic, matter of fact, minimalist, and reportage-like. American temporalities and rituals are addressed as part of everyday life and used as structuring devices in his narratives—first and foremost, the American civil religious calendar, which serves as the backbone and background for many of his texts: Valentine's Day, Fourth of July, Thanksgiving, Halloween, Christmas. These occasions mark time and the passing of time; they are occasions for celebration and remembrance that often fall short of the high expectations that are bestowed upon them, or they trigger interpersonal misunderstandings and social disintegration. Again, this demystification bespeaks the antisentimental mode. At the same time, there are also moments of drama, revenge, and retrospection. Stewart O'Nan, whether writing about matters of life or death or about the seemingly banal, is a thoroughly antisentimental writer.

Third, although unsentimental, O'Nan's writing can be characterized as literary care work. Neither heroizing nor romanticizing his characters, O'Nan is more subtle, creating full-fledged fictional worlds around ordinary people who, he suggests, are deserving of such attention in literary representations, be it an elderly widow (*Emily, Alone*), a manager of a fast food restaurant about to be closed down (*Last Night at the Lobster*), or a middle-aged couple on the verge of bankruptcy (*The Odds*). O'Nan's care work is precisely not to focus only on the big dramas and exceptional ruptures in people's lives that tend to invite dramatization (he does that, too) but to pay close attention to the everydayness of these lives being led by average people under at times grueling conditions and to witness their endurance and resilience—as well as their failures. In doing so, he connects to an earlier realist tradition in American literature that has programmatically called for focusing on "the common, average man."[10] The latter "man" in Stewart O'Nan's work is taken to be more inclusive: he has invented many exceptional female protagonists in his writing. While O'Nan does not emphasize differences of race, class, and gender, they are always co-present in his works. His focus is mostly on primary relationships of care and at times neglect: between lovers and friends, parents and children, among siblings, in-laws, and neighbors. Hence, care is also often a theme of his books. How do people care or fail to care for each other? How do they cope with breaches of trust, loss of faith, disloyalty, and guilt? What can be forgiven and what will remain an obstacle—and at what cost? At times O'Nan has been "accused of coldness, of cruelty" toward his characters, as his books "offer none of Irving's Dickensian comforts, no layers of Victorian era Turkish delight to sweeten their horrors";[11] yet the at times palpable detachment in O'Nan's writing is a respectful rather than a dissecting distance, a reserve that refrains from manipulating and pandering to his audience in all too obvious ways. His works call for the fullest readerly investment, yet they may not suggest or insist on a particular kind of "preferred reading" (Stuart Hall's term).[12]

These three dimensions of O'Nan's work—the everyday gothic, the examination of American mythologies, and the literary care work—can be identified (in more overt or more subtle ways) in most of his writings and allow for a first characterization and contextualization of Stewart O'Nan's literary worlds even as this is by no means an exhaustive classification of his oeuvre.

O'NAN'S DEBUT NOVEL, *Snow Angels* (1994)—the book that O'Nan himself recommends readers unacquainted with his work to pick up first (see the interview in the appendix)—exhibits these three dimensions, and I want to exemplarily point them out. The novel is based on O'Nan's story "Finding Amy" from his previous short story collection. Like the preceding publication, his novel was also awarded a prize, winning the Pirate's Alley Faulkner Society's first Gold Medal for Best Novel. Set in small-town Pennsylvania in 1974, the story has been described as a "tragedy in the heartland" and showcases many of O'Nan's hallmarks, such as a small-town setting, a lower-middle-class cast of characters, and the theme of trauma.[13]

The novel unfolds two parallel plots, one dealing with fourteen-year-old Arthur (Arty) Parkinson, whose parents are getting a divorce, and the other with Annie Marchand, Arthur's former babysitter and the mother of little Tara. Dedicated to singer Kurt Cobain, who died the year the novel was published, *Snow Angels* has a dark quality to it (some reviewers, in fact, found the novel too dark[14]), and it starts with shots—shots ringing out in the distance as the high school orchestra, with Arthur playing the trombone, rehearses on the football field for their next appearance. The shots that disrupt the rehearsal are the shots that kill Annie Marchand. As the novel opens by seemingly giving away its dramatic ending, it also indicates that the story about to unfold is not a whodunit but rather a complicated tale of a man killing his former wife. Tragedy hits Butler, Pennsylvania, as lovers become strangers or, worse, enemies, and the novel details in retrospect how this tragedy came about.

Annie had been living apart from her estranged husband, Glenn, for almost a year at this point and does not want to reconcile with him. Glenn, while being devoted to Annie and their daughter, Tara, is also battling depression and has become zealously religious. He has moved back in with his (adoptive) parents while his obvious compulsive psychological condition remains unattended. Annie, for her part, has tried to move on with her life; she has an affair with Brock—her girlfriend's partner—and relies on her mother to help her take care of her daughter, as she herself is prone to lose her temper and hurt her child. Annie, although in the end murdered by Glenn, is not set up as simply a victim of patriarchal violence. Quite the contrary, her behavior toward Tara exhibits her own demonic streak as she is overwhelmed by the pressure of single parenthood and work shifts and is neglectful of her daughter. Energies of despair and (self)destruction run wild, discharge in domestic violence, and ultimately take a turn for the worst. The everyday gothic, over long stretches characteristic of the novel's atmosphere and mood, emanates from the uncanny psychological shallows of misery and trauma. The whole town, Arthur, looking back on his childhood, would note, was a "mystery" (16). It is this specific kind of atmosphere that will become even more intense in O'Nan's oeuvre over the years.

All of the characters' lives are determined by a lack of perspective induced by different forms of abandonment leading to economic problems and psychological stress. The two families who split up in the book (Glenn and Annie Marchand as well as Arthur's parents) are confronting their downward economic mobility (not having been very far "up" to begin with) and their loss of a home on top of the pain of separation. Annie does not know how she will be able to pay for the rent, and Arthur's father is embarrassed to show his son his new apartment, a room with rugs, a sleeping bag, and no kitchen (125). Arthur and his mother move into a run-down complex with a defunct heating system. Hence, the notion of (individual) self-realization is severely hampered by material conditions and turns out to be an illusion for those who work jobs in the service sector—in restaurants, hospitals, a senior citizens' home, where they perform the care work *for others* and are poorly valued for doing so. As someone comments on Brock: "He cleans bedpans for a living" (134). O'Nan's literary care work thus points to the absence of proper care in the lives of his characters and examines how, in a culture that champions fantasies of the American dream, people often seem to be unable to take care of themselves and of each other in intimate relations in most basic ways. American myths of social mobility and the good life seem to be deconstructed and exposed throughout the novel as literally worlds apart from the characters featured in the novel living in small-town middle America who are concerned with just making ends meet: Will the car start in the morning so she can get to work on time? What if it does not? Will there be food for dinner? And will the paycheck last to the end of the month? Such are the concerns of O'Nan's characters in *Snow Angels*. Inadvertently, all of these minor dramas revolving around scarcity, deprivation, and neglect ultimately culminate in one major tragedy.

Through Arthur's flashbacks and a second narrative strand focusing on Annie, the reader learns about Tara's sudden disappearance. It is Arthur and his friend Warren who find the girl's dead body in a lake near her house, where she drowned. In the end, a retraumatized Glenn kills Annie as he blames Tara's death on Annie's neglectful behavior. To Arthur it seems that adults in crisis (his own mother included) act more like teenagers than the teenagers themselves, and the novel concludes with his realization that, however paradoxically, love and hate are twin emotions and are at times intricately intertwined. As the adults in the novel fail to take care of their children, Annie of Tara and Arthur's mother and father of Arthur, the novel almost displays a role reversal: It is Arthur who tugs his mother in when she returns from a night out with her friends: "I'd look in and make sure the covers were on her, and the next morning let her sleep while I cooked breakfast" (119). Clearly, he also temporarily experiences the sense of abandonment and neglect that characterizes the life of some of the other characters. In that light, it seems almost ironic that Annie had once been his babysitter. After he has found Tara's corpse in the lake, Arthur receives quite a bit of attention at home, among his friends, and at school, and he comments on this sudden shift and on his response to it: "Though both their sympathy and my grief were confused and would never connect, none of it was false. I would try not to question this gift." (176).

While the two plots in *Snow Angels* converge around the theme of loss and separation, they wildly, almost chiastically diverge at the end: Annie's death stands in stark contrast to Arthur's first date and romantic first kiss with Lila Raybern. Unlike little Tara, teenaged Arthur survives the breakup of his parents' marriage, and his parents do too. Yet the novel's ending remains ambiguous as it projects both a note of hope for Arthur's future (we have already learned that the adult Arthur is "comfortably divorced"; 13) and the realization that Arthur, too, will grow up to have the kinds of existential emotions that he had seen as a boy witnessing his parents' separation: "Because though it was already happening to me, I could not see how I would ever come to hate the people I loved. Yet at the same time I could do nothing to stop it, and that would not change for a very long time" (305).

The novel is almost elegiac in tone; its poetic title allows for multiple meanings: it may refer to the snow angel Glenn makes beside his daughter's grave but possibly also to himself as avenging angel and to Tara and Annie, who in the end are both buried beneath the snow. As Stewart O'Nan's first novel, *Snow Angels* is, from Arthur's perspective, a novel of initiation as he encounters and questions the meaning of love and death. In addition, the novel moves beyond Arthur's boyish consciousness and reveals the ways in which the characters are living their lives in the middle-American milieu of a depleting system that drains them of their capabilities of the care they mean to give to their families and friends. For this reason, they are well deserving of our empathy.

IN WHAT FOLLOWS, I discuss eleven of Stewart O'Nan's novels in depth, and I for the most part pair them in order to identify narrative patterns and topics, thus providing a basic structure for this book. These novels are *A Prayer for the Dying* (1999) (chapter 2); *The Night Country* (2003) and *Songs for the Missing* (2008) (chapter 3); *The Speed Queen* (1997) and *The Good Wife* (2005) (chapter 4); *Last Night at the Lobster* (2007) and *The Odds* (2012) (chapter 5); the trilogy *Wish You Were Here* (2002), *Emily, Alone* (2011), and *Henry, Himself* (2019) (chapter 6); and *West of Sunset* (2015) (chapter 7). The novels are addressed not in chronological order but in terms of thematic unity, shared concerns, and literary technique. As this volume is the first book-length study of Stewart O'Nan's writings, the conclusion offers an overview of those texts that, for sheer lack of space, I cannot discuss in detail.

Chapter 2 is dedicated to one of Stewart O'Nan's few historical novels, *A Prayer for the Dying* (1999). Set in post–Civil War Wisconsin, it bears characteristics of the western and can perhaps best be classified as a historical noir-western. The text features a Civil War veteran, Jacob Hansen, as a protagonist who is confronted with a diphtheria outbreak in his community and who is introduced, contoured, addressed, and evoked by a second-person narrator. The novel also gestures toward other texts by O'Nan that address the lingering trauma of war, such as *The Names of the Dead* (1996), which deals with a Vietnam veteran who has returned home only to find his life falling apart, and the World War II novel *A World Away* (1998) (see the conclusion).

Chapter 3 discusses *The Night Country* (2003) and *Songs for the Missing* (2008). In placing these two books next to each other, we can identify the gothic mode as a specific representational strategy in O'Nan's work. While *The Night Country* is (almost) a straightforward ghost story of gothic horror with narrators speaking to us from their graves, *Songs for the Missing* uses gothic elements in a more subtle way—as a kind of everyday gothic—to probe the impact of a young woman's disappearance on her family and friends.

In chapter 4 the two novels *The Speed Queen* (1997) and *The Good Wife* (2005) both feature female lead characters who have to deal with the American prison system from the perspective of a perpetrator (*The Speed Queen*) and of a relative on the outside (*The Good Wife*). Whereas the former is a fast-paced thriller that in flashbacks makes use of the conventions and literary props of the road novel and is reminiscent of films such as *Natural Born Killers* (1994) or *True Romance* (1993), the latter covers the rather monotonous and uneventful life of a wife whose husband is serving a decades-long prison sentence.

Chapter 5 discusses the two shorter novels *Last Night at the Lobster* (2007) and *The Odds: A Love Story* (2012). Largely written in a social realist idiom, both texts share the theme of economic disparity and precariousness under late capitalism and have been described by the author as "companion pieces."[15] While *Last Night at the Lobster* is set at a fast food restaurant about to be closed down and introduces us to the individual characters, workers in the service sector whose fates are impacted by this decision taken at a distant company board, *The Odds,* whose setting is the very popular honeymoon travel destination Niagara Falls, presents the reader with unconventional attempts to resist private bankruptcy and marriage breakdown.

Chapter 6 studies the masterful trilogy of the Maxwell family, which began with *Wish You Were Here* (2002)—still one of the most formally innovative and complex novels by O'Nan to date, a novel that encompasses a family reunion and vacation at Chautauqua Lake. The trilogy continues with *Emily, Alone* (2011) and concludes, for the time being, with a prequel to both, *Henry, Himself* (2019). The trilogy on the upper-middle-class Maxwell family in Pittsburgh, novels of manners, of sorts, spans three generations and several decades of American history. It explores the family as a primary social institution, as the site of unresolved conflicts, troubled intimacies, and often unspoken expectations and disappointments—and explores how these constellations are reproduced with every new generation.

Chapter 7 examines *West of Sunset* (2015)—O'Nan's Hollywood novel set in the late 1930s, the golden age of the dream factory. The book portrays the last years in the life of the writer F. Scott Fitzgerald, author of *The Great Gatsby,* as he, increasingly frail, seeks to tap into his former Hollywood fame and to start over amid turbulences in his life, in his country, and in the world. Battling the demons of alcoholism without much success, feeling torn between his obligations toward his family (his wife, Zelda, is in a mental institution) and the longing for a fresh start out West, and frantically trying to finish his manuscript, O'Nan's Fitzgerald ultimately succumbs to his illness.

Chapter 8 concludes the study with a short overview of the writer's oeuvre and a brief summary of the findings.

The appendix includes an original interview with Stewart O'Nan conducted for this publication that adds yet another perspective on the works discussed in this volume; as may befit a book of this kind, the author gets to have the last word.

CHAPTER 2

Noir-Western and Morality Play

A Prayer for the Dying

A Prayer for the Dying (1999) can easily be considered one of the literary jewels in O'Nan's oeuvre. Critics agree that with the publication of his fifth novel, "apprenticeship is over."[1] The novel is a superb example of how O'Nan uses, expands, and reconfigures well-known genres, such as the western and the gothic tale. The book has been called an "apocalyptic anti-western" and "a sinister gothic mystery."[2] It is also a novel addressing the aftermath of the American Civil War and an example of what Priscilla Wald in a different context has called an "outbreak narrative."[3] In what follows, all of these generic frameworks are examined. What holds the novel together in the end, I suggest, is the protagonist's quasi-religious quest.

The novel is set in the small town of Friendship, Wisconsin, six years after the war has ended. Jacob Hansen, the protagonist, is the town's sheriff and undertaker as well as minister. At times, "it can be too much" (4). He is a veteran of the Civil War and now lives with his wife, Marta, and their daughter, Amelia, still a baby, in what at first glance seems to be an idyllic setting. This is how the novel begins:

> High summer and Friendship's quiet. The men tend the shimmering fields. Children tramp the woods, wade the creeks, sound the cool ponds. In town, women pause in the heavy air of the millinery, linger over bolts of yard goods, barrels of clumped flour. The only sound's the freight drumming through to the south, tossing its plume of cinders above the treetops, the trucks clicking a mile off. Then quiet, the buzz of insects, the breathless afternoon. Cows twitch and flick.

You like it like this, the bright, languid days. (3)

This initial pastoral scenery presents the prototypical fantasy of U.S. settler colonialism: the successful cultivation of the land that Henry Nash Smith, in his classic *Virgin Land: The West as Symbol and Myth,* refers to as the "garden myth," which is here exemplified by men in the fields along with women going about their domestic work, children playing, and tranquil cows while the "machine in the garden"—that is, the train—is still at a remote distance.[4] Yet this hyperbucolic, idyllic setting is deceptive, and the town soon will turn into a hellish place, a purgatory of sorts. Even as the narrative recurrently evokes similar peaceful, almost picture-book moments (20), the course of events will ultimately destroy any hope for peace, harmony, and physical and spiritual well-being. After the horrors of the Civil War, it is suggested, there can be no return to a state of innocence and equanimity, let alone happiness—not for Jacob, in any case.

Soon Jacob has to deal with two mighty foes: he has to confront his inner demons (arising from his traumatic war experiences) and those that afflict his town: disease and fire. When an unknown man, presumably a former soldier turned tramp, is found dead (7), the outward signs of the dead body quickly point to a contagious infection, and when an out-of-town woman, Lydia Flynn, turns up sick and delirious shortly thereafter (15) with similar symptoms ("She's like the soldier, her eyes sunken in violet pits, cheeks creased and hollow"; 39), it is another foreboding hint at what is to come. Reluctant to give up the fantasy of his pastoral utopia, Jacob is tempted to ignore the signs of impending catastrophe ("you know you're trying not to think of the soldier, of the awful possibilities"; 43). The third encounter with the disease is the stricken Clytie, a horse, which he has to shoot (49). For a while he still clings to hope: "Worry rolls inside you like a wheel. What's the connection between Clytie and the tramp? The woman from the Colony? How long till it hits town? Or will it pass by, suddenly veer into the fields like a twister?" (51). It will not. Instead the epidemic hits the town of Friendship with full force. The death toll rises with every passing day, and the disease also does not spare Jacob's own family. At the literal center of the novel (chapter 4 of 7), Jacob's little daughter Amelia falls ill (72) and dies. His wife also starts to show symptoms.

The cleverly devised narrative does not clearly mark the death of his wife, indicating that Jacob himself refuses to acknowledge it. In fact, Jacob does not even tell anybody of his family's sickness. The people in Friendship with whom he interacts—the doctor, his deputy, the residents—are all led to believe that his wife and child are at home and still in good health. Jacob is not prepared to let them go, and for a while he even pretends that they are still alive: "Marta's waiting for you in the dark with Amelia. . . . After dinner Marta plays the melodeon and the two of you sing. She falls off the stool but you prop her up, set her feet on the pedals, her fingers on the keys, help her find middle C. . . . Later, under the covers, Marta's skin warms to yours, and you lay there with your arms around her, reciting prayers enough for all of Friendship" (135, 140).

Reviewers have commented on the unsettling quality of the scenes of necrophilia in the novel that include Jacob having intercourse with his dead wife. They are clearly reminiscent of the Southern gothic tradition and texts such as William Faulkner's "A Rose for Emily" (1930). As a soldier and as an undertaker, Jacob has been spending a lot of time with the dead, during the war and after. The novel painstakingly describes the care he takes in preparing and arranging the dead for burial. He has seen so many dead bodies—in the war and in the morgue—that he seems to have normalized living in their presence. Thus, for the protagonist, the dichotomous difference between the living and the dead seems to be suspended, and his "prayers enough for all of Friendship" include the living, the dying, and the dead. Aside from the literary gothic tradition, O'Nan explicitly names as an influence on *A Prayer for the Dying* Michael Lesy's classic nonfiction book *Wisconsin Death Trip* (1973), which chronicles, above all, the omnipresence of death in nineteenth-century small-town America: in childbirth, through suicide, and by disease, abuse, and violence of various kinds. Lesy's book is based on photographs taken by Charles Van Schaick in a small Wisconsin community between 1890 and 1910. Lesy first came across these pictures at the Wisconsin Historical Society, which to this day has a collection of Van Schaick's pictures in its archives. These representations of the grim side of rural life, in which death was an everyday occurrence, have thoroughly informed *A Prayer for the Dying*, and the standard edition of the novel has a photograph from the Van Schaick collection on the cover. The scenes of death and of corpses that O'Nan describes at times specifically use an aesthetics modeled on photographic conventions of the time: when Jacob arranges his wife and daughter around the table, on a stool or in bed, the reference to nineteenth-century postmortem photography becomes obvious.

In terms of its topic—an epidemic outbreak—the novel echoes a literary tradition of narratives of epidemics dating back in English literature all the way to Daniel Defoe's *History of the Plague in London* (1722) and in American literature to Charles Brockden Brown's *Arthur Mervyn* (1799) about the yellow fever epidemic in Philadelphia in 1793. In twentieth-century American literature, Willa Cather's *One of Ours* (1922), William Maxwell's *They Came Like Swallows* (1937), and Katherine Ann Porter's *Pale Horse, Pale Rider* (1939) come to mind, all of which are concerned with the 1918 pandemic often referred to as the Spanish flu. Stewart O'Nan's novel also resonates with Albert Camus's *The Plague* (1947), from which it takes one of its epigraphs: "There is no escape in a time of plague. We must choose to either love or to hate God." This motto resonates with allusions to the many biblical stories of human suffering and skepticism about God's grace in the face of disaster and thus, on an abstract level, addresses the question of theodicy.

As the epidemic spreads, Jacob watches the town around him die. At first the doctor, Doc Guterson, wants to avoid a panic and beseeches Jacob to keep his suspicions to himself until they are certain what disease they are faced with, despite the fact that he early on, at the end of the first chapter, already correctly diagnoses it as diphtheria (26). Only in the second half of the novel (chapter 5) is a quarantine officially imposed, and a sign is posted at the town limits: "Town Sick" (105). By then, the doctor himself has been infected and is dying. Predictably, there is resistance to the quarantine, and some residents of Friendship try to escape to neighboring settlements or seek to receive visitors from the outside. Jacob and his helpers eventually have to resort to violence against fellow residents and animals in order to maintain the quarantine and to destroy contagious matter. This is when the narrative becomes more explicitly gruesome: "Burn down houses. Burn down barns filled with dead cattle, coops filled with chickens. At Bjornsons, one hen isn't dead and tries to fly, its feathers burning. You hit it with your shovel until it stops" (124). In the process of burning down the houses of deceased epidemic victims as a precautionary measure, Jacob even casually burns one person alive:

> Yesterday you burned down a house with someone in it. Doc asked you to. It was the Winslets, out west of town. . . . You didn't like it, you said, but you brought the crew out, soaked the baseboards with kerosene, and stood there watching it, angry with everyone but the millhands who'd been pressed into service. You thought of Roland in bed under dirty sheets, and how you'd want to be found. And while you were standing there fuming, you all saw the figure in the attic window, in the invalid room, banging at the glass with her frail bare arms until it fell and shattered on the porch roof. The slow aunt from Eau Claire, you'd all forgotten her. You'd done such a good job there was no chance. She screamed but she was too old to jump, and soon smoke filled the window, the roof collapsed, and sparks boiled up into the sky. Later, you found her in the basement, light as a husk. (152–53)

Overall, Jacob considers Friendship's state of exception "as if this is the war again" (151), as things unfold "like Kentucky during the war" (158). Collateral damage, such as the "slow aunt" in the attic, calls into question his Christian faith and his ethics, as containing the epidemic takes priority over the humane treatment of the sick and needy. Due to the quarantine, Friendship comes to resemble a town under siege, both from within and from without. More and more, the destruction of the town and the psychological disintegration of the protagonist seem to mirror each other. In our time, Jacob would probably have been diagnosed with posttraumatic stress disorder as a result of his war experiences and what the war did to him.[5] In the novel, his war trauma is literally rekindled, first by the diphtheria outbreak, then by the wildfires that will eventually consume much of the town. Priscilla Wald and others have argued that "outbreak narratives" can usually be read symptomatically as pointing to larger cultural, social, and political dynamics in moments of crisis.[6] In *A Prayer for the Dying,* the plague, apart from Jacob's own interpretation that it is a punishment for his sins (the origin of this externalization or projection is revealed only on the last pages), is also a comment on the overall incommensurability of inflicting violence with administering care, a point to which I will return. Clearly, in this novel, there is no "regeneration through violence" as in the classical western literature Richard Slotkin discusses in his magisterial study of the same title.

A Prayer for the Dying shares a rare feature with novels such as *Absalom, Absalom!* (1936) by William Faulkner, *Buffalo Soldiers* (1993) by Robert O'Connor, and *Bright Lights, Big City* (1984) by Jay McInerney: it is written in the second person ("you"). This narrative technique creates an imploring and ominous tone and also establishes a complicity between the protagonist and the reader. In fact, second-person narration gestures toward a convergence of the protagonist and the reader, "which alternatively signals personal involvement with the protagonist and the evasion of subjectivity" altogether, as Monika Fludernik notes, especially when we consider "you" also to be a non-specific, generalized form of address.[7] In O'Nan's novel, readers are in this way drawn into the story and kept alert while the protagonist is cast as alienated and traumatized—an evasive, unstable subject, so to speak. The "you"-address is somehow connected to the advice and self-help genres and implies the quality of orality and instructions given to someone in need of guidance. And yet there is still another way in which we can account for the second-person narrator. Could it be, as Tim McCarthy suggests, that "'you' is Jacob talking to himself, watching his way, eying his past, conversing with his conscience"?[8] It may just be "Jacob wrestling his angel."[9] In a religious sense, the narrative refers to a dispute between reason and faith, or, in a psychological sense, the narrative voice reflects the split subject as Jacob acts in the narrative in response to the internal and external "twin horrors" involving the past war and the present diphtheria-related destruction.[10] His care for the corpses appears to be his way of reconciling this contradiction: "If there's anything your jobs have taught you, it's to take death seriously, give it the same respect as love" (10). The unreliability of the "you"—of Jacob—is revealed in its entirety only at the very end.

This somewhat experimental quality of the novel in terms of its narrative structure and voice fits well with a trend of reworking the old formula of the western; over the last decades many new and often quite stylized variations of the western have appeared in film and television (recent examples include *The Hateful Eight, Hell or High Water, Deadwood,* and *Godless*) as well as literature, among them Cormac McCarthy's novels; additionally, older texts like John Williams's 1960 novel *Butcher's Crossing* (also set after the Civil War) have been rediscovered. *A Prayer for the Dying* presents its own variation of the post–Civil War western, a noir-western, to be precise, and I draw on Jane Tompkins's work on the defining features of the genre to discuss the novel's adherence to and diversion from the generic formula.

Jane Tompkins has pointed to the preoccupation with death as one of the foundational features of the western; she speaks of "the genre's love affair with death" ("Death is everywhere in this genre"), which occurs in a great variety of forms (shootouts, raids, starvation, accidents).[11] The ubiquity of death in O'Nan's novel is tied to a centripetal setting that becomes increasingly claustrophobic and offers no room for a way out, let alone expansive adventures in a "frontier spirit." Even Jacob's final plan to stop the train coming through in order to save the remaining thirty town residents from the quickly approaching fire fails: the train derails, and all of its passengers die. Jacob, who was not on the train, is the sole survivor. He has utterly failed to keep his family and his community safe; in fact, he has inadvertently led the survivors to their deaths: early on, before the outbreak, he dissuaded his wife from leaving with their daughter, and he was complicit in not making the first diphtheria cases public. As a consequence, none of Friendship's residents escape; this certainly is an unsettling lack of apprehension, sense, and insight, dismantling the myth of the western hero and his benevolent heroism.

The initial characterization of the protagonist already diverges in obvious ways from that of a western hero. For one thing, Jacob does not like horseback riding. Horses are part of the iconic setup of the genre, one of its indispensable props ("you can't have a Western without them"[12]). Instead, Jacob prefers to ride on what could be called an early version of the bicycle, a vehicle that was just becoming popular around the time the novel takes place: "That's the one thing you'll admit is strange about you: you don't like to be around horses anymore. It's understandable, having had to eat them during the siege, to burrow into their warm, dead guts for cover, but you don't talk about that, or only to Marta, who'd never let it slip" (5–6). One would imagine that a western hero on a bicycle is funny and produces comic relief, but in this noir novel it does not. It instead conveys Jacob's postwar melancholia and lack of resolve: "After the war, you lost the will to fight, the interest in getting your way in little things" (28).

The only showdown—another typical ingredient of the western genre—the novel stages is that between Jacob and a circus driver who wants to pass through the quarantined town. When Jacob refuses, the man offers him a bribe. Jacob loses his temper and literally strong-arms him into compliance. As the circus procession turns around, one member of the crew dares to resist: "The other drivers fix you with a glare, which you return expertly, daring them to say a word, spit, anything. None of them do, except the elephant, who leaves a single cannonball of a dropping as he swings around; it raises a puff of dust, then sits there like an insult as the tinny music fades" (132). As the elephant literally "gives a shit," Jacob and his deputy are left stunned and appalled. The elephant certainly is not a standard prop of the western, and it introduces a glimpse of vaudeville to the novel, a form of entertainment that will rise to popularity in the next decades and will also feature Wild West shows (most notably that of Buffalo Bill). Here we find Jacob gazing after the elephant as some sort of exotic and bizarre apparition, something entirely out of place—perhaps as bizarre as a cowboy on a bicycle.

When the western genre originally took shape, Jane Tompkins argues, it sought to replace the dominant discourse of Christianity with a new ethics of (male) individualism, self-reliance, and accepted and legitimated forms of retaliatory violence. As a mode of cultural production, the western also responded to earlier forms of popular culture and sought to replace them: "The female, domestic, 'sentimental' religion of the best-selling women writers—Harriet Beecher Stowe, Susan Warner, Maria Cummins, and dozens of others—whose novels spoke to the deepest beliefs and highest ideals of middle-class America, is the real antagonist of the Western. . . . The Western *answers* the domestic novel."[13] The precarious, idealized, yet marginalized domestic space in classic westerns Tompkins here points to is also referenced in O'Nan's novel in an early description of Jacob's home and hearth that explicitly names one of the domestic novelists Tompkins mentions: "Still, you think, snap beans for supper. You'll coax Marta into singing while you play the melodeon, and after Amelia's down, the two of you will read to each other from Mrs. Stowe until you reach the end of the chapter."[14]

This reference to Harriet Beecher Stowe and, it can be assumed, to her bestselling novel *Uncle Tom's Cabin* (1852) hints not only at Jacob's longing for some marital bliss as an antidote to his traumatic war experience but also at the historical context of nineteenth-century evangelicalism and reminds us of the religious theme that permeates *A Prayer for the Dying* (54–55, 64, 75–76, 94, 123, 195). Jacob's own religious education is repeatedly linked to his mother, a devoted Christian who died with her hands folded over her Bible (94). After all,

Jacob is not only the sheriff and the undertaker but also the pastor of Friendship. As the epidemic becomes rampant, he struggles with the composition of a sermon he anticipates no one will attend. Biblical allusions can also be made out regarding the plot in other instances: to stories about the plague as God's punishment (for example, in Gen. 19, the story of Sodom and Gomorra, or in 2 Sam. 24:14–16). But who would be the sinner who has brought such tragedy over the town of Friendship? In a religious interpretive framework, there is reason to assume that the invisible power Jacob is up against may not only be bacteria but also God himself. Jacob partially perceives and receives the unfolding of events as a punishment inflicted upon him as a test of his faith. At the end of the novel the protagonist reveals that this may all be about a mortal sin that he committed during the war: "You remember tending to the little Norwegian, taking great care with him. They all thought he was your friend, that the two of you were inseparable, the way you looked after him, so devoted. You wouldn't let anyone touch him. You buttoned his sleeves so they didn't see the marks on his arms where you stripped the meat off when they were asleep. You said a prayer after you buried him, made another promise to God, instantly became a different man. But did you really change? You thought you had. Now you don't know" (194).

Jacob's prayer for the dying is his prayer for the dying/dead Norwegian whom he pretended to care for while in fact eating him. This, of course, adds another ugly aspect to Jacob's strange relation to the dying and the dead. Cannibalism, although sometimes addressed, is certainly not a fixture of the western formula (nor a common topic in historical descriptions). The hypocrisy of Jacob's care work unfolds in his narrative of failed redemption, in which he has literally failed everyone. Unlike Stowe's Tom, he will not be a martyr for a cause but a survivor, despite having unpardonably sinned. In that sense, *A Prayer for the Dying* is rather the *inversion* of the martyr narrative and seems to call for disgust instead of empathy on the part of the reader. In the words of O'Nan, it is a "Christian existential horror book."[15] In this vein, it has been called "the Book of Job minus the happy ending."[16] Jacob is a multiple survivor—of the war, of the epidemic, of the fire—and the sole survivor of Friendship. No trace but ashes and no human being are left from the novel's initial idyll, as the whole place comes to resemble a wasteland. At the end, all that is left for him to do is bury the bodies, "the rest of Friendship": "You still feel a duty to them—owe it, really—and you climb the engine again and bring back the shovel. It's hard but the dirt's loose, and you've got gloves. You're used to work. In Kentucky you did this for weeks" (193). Hence, finally, Jacob is back on the battlefield of the Civil War. Perhaps he never left, or the war never ended. Thus, we are left with images of the frontier that are saturated with destruction, stasis, and depletion instead of new beginnings, growth, and completion as the frontier myth would have it.

In this noir-western about an epidemic outbreak, Stewart O'Nan infuses the western formula in its historical setting with elements of the gothic. Hence, the book has been called "a cross between Stephen Crane and Stephen King."[17] At the center of the tale he places a troubled protagonist who realizes that, even as he is physically saved from death, he cannot save himself (195), nor can he save others. He learns that "you can't bargain with God, buy Him with pieties . . . even with the best intentions, even with all of your thoughtful sermons and deep feelings and good work, you can't save anyone, least of all yourself" (195). At the end of the novel he chooses to remain in Friendship (his "home") in the company of the dead rather than begin a new life elsewhere among the living. This seems to carry quite an ambiguous message: it may be seen as his defeat as a pastor but taken as showing his specific resilience as an individual since he does not give in to resignation; his carrying on may refer to an extra strong self-reliance or his inability to perform a fresh start due to his being utterly lost in the realm of death, an outcast among the living.

The next chapter continues to examine in a wider scope the important role of the gothic and its broad range in O'Nan's work.

CHAPTER 3

Gothic Horror and Everyday Gothic

The Night Country and *Songs for the Missing*

The two texts covered in this chapter present different manifestations of the gothic mode in Stewart O'Nan's writing. *The Night Country* (2003) is a tale of gothic horror featuring supernatural elements, even including ghostly narrative voices. *Songs for the Missing* (2008) explores the everyday gothic in a neorealist fashion, so to speak; the uncanny here resides in an unaccounted-for absence rather than in a ghostly presence. Both novels are set in small towns (in Connecticut and Ohio, respectively) that are deemed "boring" by the teenaged protagonists who live in them ("this is the suburbs; nothing happens here" [*The Night Country;* 4]; "every night they fought a war against boredom and lost" [*Songs for the Missing;* 3]), and who cannot wait to leave them behind. However, in these supposedly uneventful settings, mysterious things do happen—at times even with fatal consequences.

The Night Country is a contemporary ghost story set in the suburban town of Avon, Connecticut. It is also a story narrated by ghosts, the ghosts of three teenagers—foremost Marco, "the quiet one," with Toe and Danielle assisting, as it were. The three ghosts roam through the town, peek into houses, and tell us what they see. They relate the events of the narrative, and they also chatter with each other. All three of them were killed in a terrible car accident on Halloween; now they have come back to haunt the living and observe how they cope with their memories of the event (or the loss of those memories) and their feelings of survivor guilt. Kyle, who was in the car with Marco, Toe, and Danielle and who has been left disabled by the accident, is now being cared for by his mother, whereas Tim, Danielle's boyfriend and another passenger in the car, has survived the crash physically unharmed but psychologically devastated and is now suicidal. Police Officer Brooks, who was the first officer on the scene, continues to be drawn to the crash site; he is another main character that the novel fleshes out; his wife, Melissa, accuses him of having become obsessed with the accident and has since left him. Like the specters of the teenagers roaming the town, Brooks cruises the town in his police car and watches over the survivors. With Halloween—the anniversary of the car crash—approaching, all kinds of energies concentrate on the tragic event in the past and on the meaning it may have for the present. All the characters have plans for the occasion (with different agendas, it turns out), and the novel unfolds in anticipation of what is going to happen one year after the fatal accident. There is a sense of secrecy, madness, revenge, and despair in the air.

The Night Country was published on the heels of what Dina Khapaeva describes somewhat ambivalently as the 1990s "Gothic renaissance and the explosion of the horror genre," which she sees defined by "an aesthetic that is fixated on violent death."[1] The defining characteristics of this gothic trend for her are the conveying of the experience of a nightmare to the reader along with the use of an undead person (vampire, zombie, etc.) as a first-person narrator.[2] However, many scholars have pointed out that the gothic has been a durable if not timeless genre ever since it first appeared in eighteenth-century literature. Generally, "the Gothic world is fascinated by violent differences in power, and its stories are full of constraint, entrapment and forced actions. Scenes of extreme threat and isolation—either physical or psychological—are always happening or about to happen."[3] With a view to American literature and culture, Stewart O'Nan's text certainly has to be contextualized in a culture-specific tradition of the gothic dating back to Charles Brockden Brown and Edgar Allan Poe, and it can be more specifically categorized as a case of the more recent "suburban gothic" identified by Bernice Murphy: "The most characteristic narrative trope of the Suburban Gothic is, of course the revelation, time and time again, that no matter how picturesque and peaceful a neighborhood, house or family may seem on the surface, dark and usually terrible secrets lie beneath, whether of a psychological, supernatural or familial nature."[4]

This certainly holds true for O'Nan's novel—even if Avon is not made out to be all that idyllic from the very beginning. What critics have referred to as a "tasty Halloween treat"[5] is a book that is saturated with intertextual references to the Anglo-American gothic tradition. It echoes Charles Dickens's *A Christmas Carol in Prose, Being a Ghost Story of Christmas* (1843) and Shirley Jackson's gothic horror novel *The Haunting of Hill House* (1959), but also films such as George Romero's *Night of the Living Dead* (mentioned by O'Nan himself as a model; Romero, like O'Nan, is from Pittsburgh). The book's third chapter is titled "Dawn of the Dead" in reference to Romero's 1978 horror film of the same name. The fact that the accident took place on Halloween of course also evokes the horror genre, as countless horror stories in fiction and film are set around this day (most iconically, perhaps, is the *Halloween* film series). *The Night Country* furthermore references films such as *The Blair Witch Project* (1999)—another horror story involving young adults among trees—*The Shining* (1980), and *The Wicker Man* (1973) (17, 86, 226). The novel is dedicated to Ray Bradbury, whom O'Nan in an interview has called one of his first "great loves" in literature: "There was something magical about his short stories. One of my favorite books of all time is *Something Wicked This Way Comes*. I loved that book and for years I've said that I'm going to try to write something like that."[6] In view of this assertion, it is unsurprising that O'Nan, in a reverential nod to Bradbury, titled the first chapter of *The Night Country* "Something Wicked." In addition to all of these literary and filmic influences, *The Night Country* is apparently also based on a true story that Stewart O'Nan came across in a newspaper about two teenagers who narrowly escaped a fatal accident, returned to the same location a year later, and crashed their car, killing themselves;[7] the similarities to the story of O'Nan's novel seem obvious.

It should be emphasized that the novel is not generic formula fiction proper or just another simple tale of horror. For one thing, the book does not trigger the typical genre-specific reaction in its readers: "In spite of its horror-flick plot and goblin-night atmosphere, *The Night Country* is not a scary read. It is, however, a chilling one. Avon is a bucolic suburban town, where the busy production of beauty and convenience ought to demonstrate control over fate, nature and life's darker forces. Car crashes explode that sense of wealth, health and safety; they are providence's cackling guffaw."[8] It is the feeling of discomfort rather than fear that is evoked by the setting: Avon is introduced as a conglomeration of strip malls with fast food restaurants, residential streets with Halloween decorations, and "wild woods" (4) on the outskirts of town: "this is still a new England, garden-green, veined with black rivers and massacres" (4). The readers along with the residents of Avon are, in turn, addressed by the ghosts and called upon to heed their concerns: "Come then, come with us, out into the night" (3). The ghost narrators like to blur the line between the living and the dead: "It's what we always hated about Avon. The place is a fucking ghost town" (199). The latter is to be understood in both literal and metaphorical terms: the town of Avon appears to be the stage of a special kind of Halloween spectacle orchestrated by the undead teenagers, yet at the same time it seems to be a town already in decline, maybe even a dying town, haunted by the specter of its bloody New England history. The circumstance of its ghostliness may also be a symptom of the "Suburbia-Disturbia" Murphy has analyzed. Like many other tales by Stewart O'Nan, this one can be described as a narrative of decay or downfall (*Verfallsgeschichte*) both in terms of setting and plot.

The experimental technique of posthumous narration in *The Night Country* is vaguely reminiscent of William Faulkner's *As I Lay Dying* (1930) and is more generally considered to be a modernist invention; a contemporaneous example would be Alice Sebold's popular *My Lovely Bones* (2002), which is narrated in a similar vein as O'Nan's novel. Posthumous narration calls for a very specific "willing suspension of disbelief"—to use Samuel Coleridge's classic phrase—in an otherwise realistic scenario.[9] Beyond that, the book challenges the reader to keep track of who is doing the narration: O'Nan uses Marco to speak for the dead, with Toe and Danielle commenting occasionally, and allows him to access other characters' minds: ghosts, after all, know everything. The ghosts' commentary and dialogue regularly appear in brackets in the text. They present an intervention, a disruption of the narrative, in true "spirit" of the disruptive function of ghosts. Take, for instance, Tim's thoughts on Kyle and his former girlfriend, Danielle: "It's like having a kid, Tim thinks, which makes him think of Danielle and the perfect life they would have had together. (Kids? Danielle says. I don't *think* so.) He used to have Danielle, now he has Kyle" (30). In *The Night Country,* the dead, rather than being voiceless, are given narrative privileges (just like omniscient narrators) and make themselves heard in a language that is both faithful to the idiom of youth culture and at the same time also quite elegiac; both registers add to the "thick description of a social milieu" achieved in the novel.[10] In that sense, their ghostly presence is not primarily inscrutable, enigmatic, and mysterious—in fact, their voices can be considered part of the hermeneutic enterprise of the novel: to guide the reader in understanding what happened a year ago on Halloween. These ghosts appear to be playful yet at the same time "mildly malevolent," inducing the reader to wonder about their presence, their agency, and their power over the living.[11] Are they mere observers? Are they steering the plot, moving it forward? Are they manipulating the characters? And if so, what is their plan? Might they be plotting revenge, even murder? In his review of *The Night Country,* Hubert Winkels convincingly likens the ghostly narrators to the three "furies" (the Erinyes) of classical Greek mythology—goddesses of revenge and retribution who could inflict madness or illness—referring to them as "teenage furies."[12] The wrath of the furies could only be placated by the proper rituals of atonement and purification. In that sense, the ghosts of Marco, Toe, and Danielle are also asking for atonement and the proper rites that put the souls to rest, and the reader is about to find out what these are. That all of this comes to a head on Halloween is not surprising. In the contemporary American cultural imaginary, the spectacle of Halloween (which serves as a rather symbolically loaded background to the story) can perhaps be considered as fulfilling the function of a popularized death cult or a commodified mythology of sorts in the apparent absence of orthodox religious beliefs and practices. As a cultural symptom exceeding O'Nan's novel, the growing popularity and importance of Halloween in the United States (and elsewhere) has been observed by scholars to almost rival the Christmas holiday in terms of public display and spending patterns and hence also in cultural relevance.[13]

The first chapter of *The Night Country* includes a brief recounting of the accident: "There's a second in which we realize we're not going to make the curve—all of us, even the most hopeful. The sound of the road, so constant, disappears, vacuumed into black silence" (7). The following briefly shows how the characters in the novel, both dead and alive, retrace their steps to the fatal night one year ago and how all of them literally make their way back to the tree marking the site of the accident; how they remember and project upon this tragic event; and how they try to render it meaningful by seeking closure, death, or new beginnings. It is this location of the tragedy that the various narrative threads will converge upon in the end: a tree in a curve that continues to draw people and their thoughts to it, having become a shared yet private landmark of remembrance.

The first to visit the accident site that day is Nancy Sorenson, a schoolteacher, who is addressed in the novel only as "Kyle's mom" (34). Since she is taking care of him, she no longer has a paid job but still does volunteer work at the local public library (a place she thinks of as peaceful, open, and consoling); she devotedly watches the soap opera *One Life to Live,* a fixture in her daily life that helps her avoid drinking, and "wonders if everyone makes their lives a series of routines they can handle" (51). Occasionally, she dreams that Kyle, too, died in the accident ("this time there are no survivors"; 55) and finds it "a relief, this latenight dream, a reason to feel even worse, a kind of self-torture she can't avoid, though she knows she doesn't really believe in it" (55). Her son's accident has left her isolated in the town of Avon: "She's alone here, the neighbors unsure how to approach her" (76). For the occasion of the anniversary, she has put together a commemorative wreath with photographic images of the teenagers. On the anniversary, she takes it to the site of the accident. To her, it is like a visit to the cemetery or some sort of symbolic gravesite, as the "old Kyle" also died here: "She's been here before but is surprised to see how ugly the place is, how insignificant, not the great stage of a tragedy. The grass is a wrack of dust and muddied cigarette butts. Beneath the faded notebook paper and the stapled pictures, the tree seems smaller than she remembered, harmless, not a murderer" (89). At the library, she offers a Halloween reading for children, and in the evening she makes attempts at "normalizing" her relationship with her husband, "Kyle's dad": they are going out to dinner, followed by shared intimacy in bed, yet she cannot help thinking about Kyle all the time (191–94).

Most of the reviews of the novel hardly mention her, but as a kind of counterpart to officer Brooks and as the only other adult the novel fleshes out, she is an important character: she is the one who is able to mourn and to go on with her life despite its disruption, trying to bridge the past and future. She touches the tree in a gesture of reconciliation, and, unlike others, she will survive the night.

Nancy's son Kyle, the "new Kyle," is the second to reach the accident site. He had survived the accident with severe brain damage and now is partially like a "baby" (34) and is partially like "a five-year-old, [who] loves fast food and cartoons" (35)—he lives in his own world, in "Kyleland" (25). He goes to a rehab facility and has a job filling shelves and collecting carts at the Stop'n'Shop, where Tim takes care of him: "He has glasses now, held on by a black elastic band, and permanent dentures. His face is flat and lopsided. His nose and cheeks aren't real, or his forehead; only his chin is the same, and his hands. He's become someone or some*thing* else" (22). Kyle likes doing puzzles, and he likes snow and Halloween candy. "What does he dream of?" (38). Kyle has become inscrutable, even to the ghosts. "What does he know, what does he remember?" (146). Occasionally, he surprises people by being mentally more agile than is usual for him, for example, by comprehending a joke. On the night of the anniversary, he surprises everyone by being clairvoyant when he calls the police to report an accident about to happen.

The third person to the accident site is Tim, who feels stigmatized as an outsider ever since the accident: a scapegoat people blame for the deaths of their children and friends. The accident also has made him a different person, if only inwardly, and he feels that he has become "a lie" (26, 40) and a stranger—as if he had lost his rootedness and partially his sense of reality. At school, "everything's off just that much, fake. If he opened the wrong door he'd find a room full of extras having their make-up retouched. And then he thinks the opposite's true—he's the one that's unreal, a ghost walking among them, a monster in disguise, *I was a Teenage Frankenstein*" (108). Feeling utterly unhinged by the upcoming Halloween anniversary of the accident, Tim has prepared a meticulously planned suicide mission, for which he pieced together the sequence of events that would lead up to the car crash, including the music that would be playing in the car. Indeed, there is a soundtrack in the novel, so to speak, which begins with the epigraph by Kurt Cobain, "I hate myself and want to die"—setting up a gothic and suicidal mood from the very beginning—and ends with a mix CD put together by Tim dedicating selected songs to those who were in the car. The Smashing Pumpkins song "Today Is the Greatest Day" (what a nihilistic pun!) is the song Tim has chosen for himself and was, as we learn, the last song playing in the car before the crash. Officer Brooks trails him on his "mission" and finally rams Tim's car, causing both their vehicles to hit the tree, and the ghosts pull Tim over into their world to fill the ranks.

Finally, there is Brooks (or "Brooksie," as the ghosts call him), who is given the most narrative space of all the characters. He is seriously traumatized by his memory of the accident, not only because he cannot forget the sight of the teenagers' horrifically mutilated bodies but, above all, because he was chasing them for speeding when the accident occurred. In many ways the night of the accident has destroyed his life: the investigation may have covered up his responsibility for the accident, yet "everyone knows Brooks isn't the same cop he used to be" (43). He revisits the scene in his mind every night, goes through the police files, and contemplates what he could have done differently. Even after his wife has left him and he has to put their house up for sale in order to repay the mortgage, he feels that, having spent all his life in Avon, there is nowhere else for him to go and no second chance in sight: "It seems every night he goes to bed with a question: What are you going to do? And there's no answer he can see, no plan of action that will change what's happened to his life. He's fifty-three, in debt, alone, a mess, and he needs to start all over again. The impossibility of it sets his mind spinning" (98). The novel's not-so-subtle way of raising doubts about Brooks' innocence is confirmed at the end: Brooks has known all along that he alone is responsible for the fatal crash, as he accidentally bumped into the teenagers' car, causing it to veer off the road and collide with the tree. The narrative hints at this already in the first chapter, when Marco, the teenage ghost, refers to a "light . . . from the trunk" (7) at the moment of the crash. In order to make up for his lethal mistake, Brooks watches over Kyle and Tim to keep them safe. He seems to be able to read Tim's mind (they have a "connection") and thus wants to prevent his suicide on the anniversary night in order to redeem himself. Yet history repeats itself, and the officer's plan backfires: Brooks fails to get Tim to stop his car, and this time both of them crash into the same tree. Brook's death, it appears, is the "sacrifice" the ghosts "required" (226) as atonement.

A sense of inexplicable destructive doom is cast over the tale, as if there were a supernatural power at work or as if there were a weird sort of inadvertent cooperation between the ghosts and the living. Did Tim lure Brooks to the tree? Or were they both led there by the ghosts? Was Kyle spared by the ghosts because the physical and mental injuries he sustained in the crash were considered enough punishment? Are we to consider their deaths—"their shared destiny" (217)—as release or as retribution? Despite (or because of) the pain and guilt that characters have involuntarily inflicted on each other, the novel does create empathy for all the characters—for the (un)dead teenagers, for Brooks, for Kyle and his mom. Even for the "enemy" tree, as Kyle's mother calls it. "Our tree. Tim's. His" (17)—early on, the ghostly voices anticipate the ending.

Ultimately, the gothic mode can be approached from two angles: The first approach is by reading its supernatural elements as being real within the world of the text. From this would follow for *The Night Country* that we take the existence of ghosts in the narrative for granted, which is an approach to the gothic that so far has guided my discussion of the novel. The second approach in gothic literary studies explains supernatural elements by interpreting them psychologically or psychoanalytically. From this perspective, the voices of the ghosts would be considered projections, inventions, or imaginings rooted in and emerging from the unconscious of the surviving characters, Brooks and Tim, as manifestations of their survivor's guilt (and, in Brooks's case, denied responsibility) projected outward. A psychoanalytic reading certainly lends itself to understanding such gothic texts as *The Night Country*. Within this logic, the text's plot would not be driven by the ghosts of the fatally injured teenagers but by the inner demons of Brooks and Tim—that is, the return of the repressed. Hence, the repetitive returns to the crash site and their final restaging of the accident would be compulsory and death-driven rather than in any way liberating. However, repetition is also a standard strategy in psychoanalytic treatment, which considers revisiting a traumatic event to be a necessary step in the healing process that allows victims, through acknowledging the trauma, ultimately to find closure. In *The Night Country*, none of the survivors actually are in psychological care or have their nightmares treated professionally in any way. Brooks is back at work, pretending that he is fine (which he clearly is not); Tim is back at school, feeling alienated from his family and his surroundings. He only has Kyle as a "friend." Thus, their traumas are not attended to, and their repetitive behaviors do not lead to healing but rather, once again, only to death. This, of course, is quite in line with the gothic genre's focus on the past disrupting the present order, closing in on individuals and driving them into despair, madness, or death.

But the novel does not end with death. The author takes poetic license to bring the characters once again back to life. The very last chapter presents the reversal and rewinding of time and with it the sequence of events. The narrative moves from the cemetery to the emergency room to the rescue squad, to the Toyota Camry "circling the tree" (228), to the road, back to town, to Danielle ending her shift at Dunkin' Donuts and to the five exuberant teenagers looking forward to having a great Halloween. This is how we last see them: "We've just gotten out of work and we're tired because all you can find around here are shitty jobs. . . . It's late and there's nowhere to go because this town sucks so much, but we don't care. We're just a bunch of dumb kids having fun. We want the night to last forever" (229). O'Nan, rather than having the novel end with another set of corpses signifying finality, death, and despair, instead hits the reset button, as it were, by using a postmodern literary device that plays with chronology, sequence, and cause-and-effect relations. The novel thus also poses questions of determinism, choice, and contingency. In contextualizing the teenagers one final time in the city of Avon (with "shitty jobs" in a town that "sucks"), *The Night Country* also points to a structural dimension of systemic failure and small-town precariousness that goes far beyond any single accident, however terrible and tragic in its consequences. As such, the ending could be read as giving the reader a glimpse of the abyss that lies beneath the thin cover of normalcy and everyday routines—in short: a glimpse of the everyday gothic, which is fully unfolded in the second novel dealt with in this chapter.

IN *SONGS FOR THE MISSING* (2008), there are no ghosts, apparitions, or voices from beyond the grave, yet its pages are nevertheless imbued with a sense of tragedy in a subtly gothic vein. The novel is set in the summer of 2005 in the small town of Kingsville, Ohio, and narrates a missing persons case. As in *The Night Country,* the focus is on a group of teenagers. Eighteen-year-old Kim Larsen, a recent high school graduate waiting to go off to college, suddenly disappears without a trace. In the first chapter of the novel, titled "Description of the Person, When Last Seen," Kim is spending her last day in her familiar surroundings, going about her usual summer routines: giving her sister driving lessons, stopping at Dairy Queen for lunch, getting pulled over for speeding by the local sheriff, hanging out with her friends Elise and Nina and with her boyfriend J. P., and getting ready for her shift at the local Conoco's. Yet she never arrives at the gas station she works at. This is the exposition of the novel and the anticipation of its drama. The first chapter follows Kim's activities through the day, none of which seem to indicate anything out of the ordinary; then she simply vanishes. It is her mother who eventually takes the first steps to find her: "The first person her mother called was Nina. The second was J. P. The third was Connie at the hospital. The fourth was the police" (15). A missing person by definition is a person who has disappeared and whose status—dead or alive—cannot be confirmed and whose whereabouts are equally unknown. Kim, the missing person in the novel, seems to have vanished into thin air. What follows in the remaining 272 pages is not so much a mystery, a thriller, or the description of police procedural but rather an unfolding and an exploration of the everyday gothic, a narrative mode that has become one of the hallmarks of O'Nan's writing; through its use he has turned many an average all-American town into an "unhomely" place. The everyday gothic creates a somewhat mysterious lacuna or "dark area"—a term Brian McHale introduced to the study of historical postmodernist fiction but that I find equally applicable here—that resonates with the readers and produces a certain kind of discomfort about what we do not, and cannot, know.[14] The everyday gothic is often subtle; it hints at physical or psychological violence rather than explicating it at length and in detail. Above all, the everyday gothic reminds us that horror can arise in and from quotidian routines. The reader of *Songs for the Missing* follows along with Kim's family and friends while wondering—and imagining—what might have taken place. O'Nan's characters do not engage in much speculation; hence, for the readers, there is room for imagining all kinds of things to have happened to her—including the worst.

At times the everyday gothic shows points of convergence with Sigmund Freud's notion of the uncanny or unhomely (*das Unheimliche*), which occurs when something that has been previously known (and known well) becomes strange and unfamiliar, hence "unhomely"—that is, scary, threatening, and unsettling in its unexpected defamiliarization of the ordinary. With Kim's disappearance, the town seems to have become a different—an unhomely—place, less familiar, predictable, and boring than previously noted, despite all its objective sameness. The novel captures very well this uncertainty (and anxiety) on the part of the characters, who do not know what happened and are trying to balance suffering and grief with hope. In fact, in *Songs for the Missing*, the author spreads an "untearable veil of horror over every-day life" or lifts the veil of normalcy from the horror lurking beneath any notion of ontological security.[15]

Anticipation of a more formulaic mystery plot or crime procedural quickly dissipates in the novel as the narration soon focuses more on waiting than on action; it stresses the protagonists' helplessness and inability to find explanations for Kim's disappearance, making the book "the thriller equivalent of watching blood dry."[16] The agony of those left behind over Kim's whereabouts and well-being takes center stage after Kim's disappearance, and the novel roughly chronicles the life of the Larsens and Kim's friends over the course of the next two years. Following Kim's disappearance, we witness how her missing persons case moves into gear only slowly because of bureaucratic red tape—at first the police do not become active in any way as she is an adult before the law and thus merely considered a runaway. Under these circumstances, Kim's family quickly learns to use the public attention generated by the incident's media coverage to their advantage, assembling search parties of volunteers, organizing commemorative events, and advertising a reward for clues about Kim's whereabouts.

Needless to say, Kim will not return alive. On page 95 of the novel her car is found, and on page 146 the police unit switches from tracker dogs to cadaver dogs. On page 173 a corpse is found, but it turns out to be someone else's; finally, on page 270, Kim's remains are discovered by a volunteer, a woman to whom the family gives the reward. Up until then, friends, family, and the public have been involved in numerous search parties, combing every square foot of Kingsville and its vicinity. Several suspects have been scrutinized, until one man, terminally ill, comes forward to confess to a series of killings, including the abduction and murder of Kim (259, 264). After his confession, he takes his own life in the prison cell. There is, of course, a funeral for Kim, which provides some sort of closure. Yet these plot-wise relevant facts pale against what the novel is actually about: a period of uncertainty, cluelessness, helplessness, and desperation, of mourning, and, ultimately, of trying to cope with a loss that is unspeakable. In that sense, despite major differences in style and setup, *Songs for the Missing* is a kind of companion piece to *The Night Country.* The latter focuses on two days (with flashbacks) in the lives of characters who suffer from posttraumatic stress that is released in a final catastrophic event. The former, at first glance, sets up a similar situation as it meticulously chronicles hour after hour, day after day of an unfolding trauma, yet it then also accompanies its characters into a posttraumatic phase that shows the ways in which the sharp experience of loss turns into a form of remembering, a process best represented in the mode of the everyday gothic. Unlike Tim and Brooks in *The Night Country,* the characters in *Songs for the Missing* seem for the most part to find ways out of their shock and despair, however hesitantly and ambivalently at first.

Throughout the novel, the focalizer (Gérard Genette's term for third-person narration informed by character perspective only, thus presenting a limited point of view) changes with each chapter, and family members as well as Kim's girlfriends and boyfriend take turns unfolding their responses to Kim's disappearance.[17] First and foremost, it is her nuclear family—her parents and sister—who are the protagonists of the novel and whose perspective is somewhat privileged in the narrative. Her father, Ed Larsen, is a real estate agent in Kingsville: "He was a good salesman, despite the beating the market had been handing him lately, an okay coach, a decent husband and father, not a bad or incompetent man at all (he hoped), but he was not going to find her, not this way. He'd felt helpless at times in his life . . . . This was different. His usually reliable talents of hustle and attention to detail were worthless against the unknown, and he was frightened" (20).

He temporarily leaves his job to help look for Kim, spending several weeks in a hotel in Sandusky, close to where Kim's car was found. Yet he quickly becomes overwhelmed by the media attention (104): "All he wanted was a single physical job that made him feel like he was doing something" (104). His hobby is fishing, which provides him with some sort of escape from the state of exception his life has become. Kim's mother, Fran Larsen, is employed at the local hospital as a nurse. The reader follows her through the bureaucratic ordeals of dealing with the authorities, for instance, doublechecking her spelling of "Caucasian" on the missing persons police form (43). As the search for Kim intensifies, Fran becomes, as it were, the public relations manager of the family and gradually changes into a person "with a serious anchorwoman's hair-style and a tailored suit" (213); she gives public speeches on behalf of her missing daughter, organizes commemorative events, and becomes a regular media presence. This leads to some estrangement from her family. Her mechanisms for coping with Kim's disappearance include drinking wine and taking sleeping medication. Ed notices that she lies next to him as if passed out (151).

Kim's younger sister, Lindsay, is the person who saw her last before she disappeared. Due to her parents' anxieties and protectiveness, she lives in a very circumscribed world after Kim's disappearance and is constantly watched over. At the same time, she feels isolated from her peers, who now consider her "a celebrity" (163). Kim's former home seems to turn into kind of a haunted house; at one point, Lindsay indeed muses that "her friends shunned the place as if it was haunted" (109), a nod, once again, to the gothic tradition. Initially being actively engaged in the search for her sister, Lindsay increasingly longs to have her own life and the quiet routines of everyday life back.

Lindsay's driving lessons are symbolic in several ways: they are what connects her to the memory of her sister, being the last thing they did together. Kim, who was about to leave the family home to start college, clearly was the object of Lindsay's admiration and envy, as Lindsay always considered herself second to Kim (who in Lindsay's estimation is "the pretty girl"; 30. Lindsay also wonders: "if she disappeared, besides her parents, who would really miss her?"; 32). In the aftermath of Kim's disappearance, Lindsay continues to practice driving with her mother, but with her parent on the passenger seat, the car seems too small, cage-like. When she has passed the driving test, her parents do not want to let her drive on her own, increasing Lindsay's feeling of being restricted, as if she was held hostage by her parents. Longing to leave town, her family, and the drama that has become her life, she is eventually relieved to go to college. Focusing on her perspective, *Songs for the Missing* is a coming-of-age novel, with the disappearance and murder of her sister catalyzing her *rite de passage*.

Lindsay's position in the narrative indicates another important theme: the generation gap between her parents, Ed and Fran, on the one hand, and Lindsay and Kim's friends, on the other. The novel reflects a generational distance and difference—even alterity—that cannot be bridged and creates misunderstanding. *Songs for the Missing* in this way is also a generational novel that partially reveals the little (as well as the bigger) secrets between parents and children that sometimes come to the fore but more often form a kind of background noise in interactions. In the process of looking for clues to find out what happened to Kim, Ed and Fran discover things about their daughter they had not known and that, because of the strained situation, arguably become blown out of proportion: Kim had a sexual relationship with Dennis Wozniak, a decorated Marine veteran living in the neighborhood who also provided her and her friends with drugs. Because of this connection, he is targeted as a suspect, and his yard is plowed through by the police—to no avail. Overall, there is nothing out of the ordinary in the lives of Kim and her friends—they are just a group of average teenagers: "Everyone had secrets, that was life" (50); Kim's friend Nina registers the lack of anonymity in their small-town lives: "The problem was that everything was connected. One lie covered another, which covered a third, which rested against a fourth. It all went back to Kingsville being so goddamn small" (56). This statement shows how the younger generation tries to break free from the social control of their elders and feels forced to create the illusion of decency to cover what in the eyes of the older generation appears as severe disruptions of the social order and as loss of control—in short, as threatening to lay bare the shaky foundations of their shallow, petty bourgeois lives.

In addition to putting the lives of their missing daughter and her friends under the microscope, Kim's parents also begin to construct an image of Kim that is not embraced by everyone and perhaps also reveals how little they understood their daughter's true self. Lindsay, for one, strongly objects to the photograph of Kim her mother chose to put on flyers and missing person posters, a photo that shows Kim "smiling in too much lipstick like Miss America" (30). It is this photo that for Lindsay makes the whole situation unreal: "The Kim that never existed smiled out at Lindsay. The flat black-and-white combined with her ridiculous updo made the picture look dated, as if she'd been kidnapped from 1985. Above the flyer was a price list. Balloons were two dollars, ribbons three, bracelets five" (114). Lindsay considers the charity event in honor of Kim, which takes place in the context of a local sports game, as a kind of "carnival" (114).

Like the photograph chosen by her mother, Lindsay believes the song Fran has chosen for her media campaign is equally inappropriate: "The idea was to choose a song people could request and dedicate to Kim, reminding listeners that she was still missing. When Lindsay first heard the song they picked she'd shaken her head. It was from a commercial, this little kid and his grandfather chasing fireflies. It had been in the movies, it had even been on *ER*. It was the kind of mushy, overplayed song Kim hated" (118). The song is "Somewhere over the Rainbow," a 1930s song made iconic by Judy Garland in *The Wizard of Oz* (1939). The version that the novel refers to is the one by Israel Kamakawiwo'ole, who is described in the novel as "the big Hawaiian guy" who "was dead, a kind of saint in Hawaii" (118). Kamakawiwo'ole's version was first recorded in 1988 but became a chart hit only in the early 2000s (it has also been used on numerous soundtracks for films and television series and is still a popular choice for all kinds of occasions, including weddings and funerals). In Lindsay's perception, the use of this song for a missing person fundraiser seems tasteless, even if hearing it play during the ceremony presided over by Fran on the softball field affects her nonetheless. A verse of the song's lyrics also serves as the epigraph of the novel: "Someday I'll wish upon a star / . . . / That's where you'll find me." One may wonder if this is meant to be ironic since the lyrics seem quite ambiguous. Whereas some scholars of the musical film *The Wizard of Oz* have argued that the song signifies a longing for "home sweet home," others have concluded that it articulates a universal and apparently timeless childhood desire to "escape."[18] Salman Rushdie, one of the more prominent voices in that debate, also considers the song as the embodiment of "the human dream of leaving, a dream at least as powerful as its countervailing dream of roots."[19] The polysemic lyrics of the song—a centerpiece in the novel—indeed allow for different interpretations: First, Fran sees it as a tribute to her daughter and embraces it as a "song for the missing" Kim. Second, the song can be interpreted as suggesting that Kim has indeed voluntarily run away to some other place that remains undefined. Third, from the perspective of those left behind, it holds the promise of Kim's return or a reunion in an unspecified time and place, including the possibility of a reunion in the afterlife, and in this sense evokes a religious dimension as well as the possibility of Kim's death. Fourth, Lindsay, in direct contradistinction to Fran, reads "Somewhere over the Rainbow" as a tacky, overtly sentimental song that her sister would not have appreciated, confirming the general disconnect and lack of understanding between her parents and their daughters. Fifth, for Lindsay it may also resonate with her own situation of feeling stuck and wishing to escape. This interpretation corresponds with what is related in the last chapter, which is ambivalently titled "There Is No Place Like Home" (another reference to *Wizard of Oz*): Lindsay comes home from college for Kim's funeral but is gladly leaving again afterward "to her new life at school, where no one could see her sister's ghost hovering over her" (282). The quotidian presence of Kim's ghost is clearly a prominent symptom of the everyday gothic scenario the novel builds up. A sixth possible way of reading the meaning of the song's lyrics in the context of the novel, of course, is—beyond its meaning for the characters—what they signify to the reader, to whom they convey the irony, futility, and theatricality of Fran's campaign, who tellingly resorts to a commodity lacking any individual specificity in a personally fraught situation because she does not know her daughter well enough to choose anything other than a default item conventionally accepted as suitable for emotionally charged events. This may be read as an indictment of the spiritual void of contemporary American consumer culture.

Despite great efforts, all attempts to find Kim come up empty-handed time and again; the novel "thwarts our expectations for cathartic tragedy or gleeful celebration, which makes the story even more devastating. This isn't the nightmare of losing your daughter; this is the numbing reality of it."[20] Readers' expectations of a story of detection and discovery are thoroughly frustrated in *Songs for the Missing*. Whereas the novel at first indeed plays with the conventions of the detective story or whodunit, it proceeds to unfold like an anti–detective story—although in contrast to postmodern metafictional anti–detective novels (for instance, Paul Auster's *New York Trilogy*), it maintains a much higher degree of realist verisimilitude. According to Tzvetan Todorov's classic definition, a detective story "contains not one but two stories: the story of the crime and the story of the investigation."[21] In O'Nan's novel, the story of the crime can, in the end, only partially be reconstructed. Regarding motive and motivation, there is no puzzle to be solved and no explanation to be found: the perpetrator turns out to be a random person, not known to any one in town, who just happened to pick Kim as his victim (one among many, as is revealed toward the end). The violence inflicted by Kim's murderer (as well as other characters in the novel) is contingent; it does not allow for the construction of a deeper, hidden meaning or logic to it, and this makes it uncanny. No information, no explanation, no theory can shed light on Kim's death or uncover any reasons behind it. Not even the arrest and conviction of the perpetrator offer any consolation for the characters, let alone gratification for the reader. O'Nan renders "the nuances of pain, which is connected to his unwavering commitment to render the truth, no matter the consequences. . . . It's the sort of experience that reveals why we read in the first place, knowing that the sadness we find inside a book mirrors the sadness always within reach."[22] And it is the mode of the everyday gothic that allows this sadness to be communicated so effectively.

Even as all of Kim's relatives and friends are grieving their loss and struggling with her absence (quite literally, she is missing *and* being missed), the novel shows how the characters cope in one way or another, proving their resilience.

In view of the last part of the novel specifically, one reviewer has referred to the book as "self-help," as "a novel about loss and healing; a novel that acknowledges the depth of loss and the limits of healing."[23] Although some characters become self-absorbed and isolated in their grief and do not always manage to reach out to one another, with time all of them seem to be able to pull through with the help of others but also supported by rituals as well as temporal and geographic distance. Fran and Ed, Nina, Elsie, J. P., and Lindsay manage to do what the characters in *The Night Country* could not.

The text refrains from indulging in graphic descriptions of what precisely happened to Kim between her abduction and death. Whereas "rape" and "murder" are mentioned in the book (197), they are not dwelt upon, let alone recounted in any detail. Even as violence clearly is lurking underneath the surface throughout the narrative, it remains a lacuna up until the end of the novel, which instead focuses on those left behind in agony and uncertainty. The everyday gothic conveys this pain and sadness as a lingering, ubiquitous, at times overwhelming emotional state affecting not only the characters of *Songs for the Missing* but also its readers.

THE EVERYDAY GOTHIC reappears in other works by O'Nan in different guises, using various motifs: an unaccounted-for mirage (*Henry, Himself*), an(other) unsolved crime (*Wish You Were Here*), or an enigmatic encounter (*A Face in the Crowd*). Reading O'Nan's novels creates a heightened perceptivity for the unsettling mysteries and dramas that linger beneath the surface of our daily routine and are part and parcel of everyday life.

To various degrees and in varying intensity, the gothic and the everyday gothic appear in many of O'Nan's works, whether in the form of a straightforward ghost story like *The Night Country,* in subtler and more implicit ways as in *Songs for the Missing,* or in combination with other narrative formulas, as in *A Prayer for the Dying* (see chapter 2). In each case the author draws on the gothic to create "a world of doubt" that he challenges his characters—and readers—to live in, with, or through.[24]

CHAPTER 4

Inside/Outside

The Speed Queen and *The Good Wife* as Prison Novels

The prison as a central institution of American society has received renewed attention over the past decades by critics of the so-called prison industrial complex and its effects on various social groups.[1] This growing awareness is evidenced by an ever-increasing number of scholarly and popular works, and, not surprisingly, the prison experience has also resurfaced in American literature. Even before these concerns were widely voiced, Stewart O'Nan focused on the prison as an institution and made it the (partial) setting of two of his novels. Both novels, *The Speed Queen* and *The Good Wife,* do not primarily engage in social criticism; they are not protest novels in the conventional sense, yet both draw somewhat sympathetic images of those who are targeted by the American justice system, and address the nexus of justice—in the sense of justness—and the law. Both titles refer to their female protagonists, whose relationships to the legal system are very different: whereas Marjorie Standiford is a white lower-class woman who becomes a drug addict and goes on a killing spree, Patty Dickerson is the white lower-middle-class wife of an inmate serving a decades-long sentence. In addition, both novels use very different generic styles: while *The Speed Queen* is a fast-paced, tell-it-all (or almost all) first-person narrative in the confessional mode, *The Good Wife* is a less spectacular narrative in the third person operating in a slice-of-life aesthetic. Substantial portions of both novels are set in prison. Whereas Marjorie is locked up on death row when the novel introduces her, Patty, trying to make her marriage work even though her husband is behind bars, becomes a regular visitor during his years in prison.

Stewart O'Nan, somewhat ironically, wrote *The Speed Queen,* his fourth book, quite speedily in just "sixty-six days."[2] Originally, however, it was supposed to be titled "Dear Stephen King" but went to press under a different name to avoid legal action from Stephen King.[3] Still, Stephen King appears as a character in the book: it is he for whom Marjorie records her life story on tape as she is awaiting execution by way of a lethal injection on death row. She has granted King an exclusive final interview, wanting him to turn her life story into what she hopes will become a bestselling book so that her son, Gainey, is financially secure when she is gone. Although Marjorie is indeed shown working her way through what seem to be interview questions in the course of the narration, the interview situation, it turns out, is purely imagined as she is speaking on a tape recorder—Marjorie's first-person, present-tense narration is, in fact, a monologue. Each section of the novel starts as a response to one of the 150 questions the fictional Stephen King has given her to answer. The novel does not explicitly include these questions, however; readers can infer them from the answers Marjorie offers. She makes it to 114 before her time is up and her sentence is carried out. In that sense, the novel is vaguely reminiscent of Gordon Lish's *Dear Mr. Capote* (1983). Lish's book is the story of a serial killer who wants Truman Capote, the famous author of *In Cold Blood* (1965), a nonfiction novel about a brutal killing spree in Kansas in 1959, to write his biography. Yet another influence on *The Speed Queen* was, according to Stewart O'Nan, the French nouveau roman, with its experiments in narrative construction.[4]

O'Nan's "Speed Queen," Marjorie Standiford, is interested in leaving behind her story—if not much else—as a legacy and a source of income for her son. To what extent the story as told by her is a truthful account of her life remains for the listeners/readers to decide. Clearly, Marjorie Standiford is an unreliable narrator if there ever was one, and her tale is full of puzzling discrepancies. At the same time, we as readers have to fill in the blanks of a fragmented story that provides answers to questions that remain only implied, demanding considerable interpretive work for a coherent narrative to emerge. As much as finding out *what* happened, we want to know *how* it happened. Throughout the book, Marjorie claims innocence on the most absurd of grounds. She is in denial about her actions, but she is also a very self-conscious narrator. Is she playing us? Can we trust her? Even sympathize with her? Or is she merely the caricature of an American heroine gone astray, lost in a cultural imaginary of sex, drugs, and violence?

Marjorie certainly does not present herself as a victim. Her account of her life is rendered in the same matter-of-fact register, with no difference in tone or attitude regardless of whether a brutal murder or the most ordinary of incidents is recounted, as if to her they were all of equal (un)importance. Readers learn that she first grew up in rural Oklahoma in the 1970s ("The next house was a mile down the road on each side"; 10) before her family moved closer to Oklahoma City, to the outskirts of Edmond, when she was five years old. Rather than using childhood experiences as an explanation or excuse for her present misfortune, Marjorie is quick to deny that childhood trauma may be at the root of her problems: "It [my childhood] was normal. I had friends. I liked school, especially geography" (15). In contrast to her own sense of what constitutes a "normal" upbringing, several anecdotes suggest to the reader that from an early age, Marjorie's life in fact has been defined by all kinds of violence: her father once swung her around and hit her head against the television console; when she consequently fell off a chair due to, presumably, a concussion, she ends up with "a fractured skull" (18). Another time, her father accidentally ran over her mother's dog in the driveway, then simply threw the dead pet into the trash bin rather than burying him in the backyard, as he claimed. As a little girl she also witnessed her parents engaging in sexual intercourse, including S&M practices such as bondage and gagging. Marjorie's childhood also involved fighting at school (in fact, the novel discloses an instance in which Marjorie retaliates against a fellow student who had been verbally abusive, with the use of disproportionate physical violence; 29) and her own first sexual experiences at an early age (56). All of this is rendered as part of the "normal" middle-American experience and reveals the extent to which Marjorie is in denial. Somewhat ironically, Marjorie comes into contact with drugs right around the time as a new "War on Drugs" is launched by then president Ronald Reagan. In the vein of psychedelic literature, Marjorie recounts her drug experiences with provocative relish: "You want me to describe that first rush. It's like a flood. It's like standing on the front of a train flying down a mountainside. It's like you've been sick for the longest time and suddenly you're all better. You feel really lucky. It's almost funny how lucky you feel. It makes you laugh. . . . But those first few hours, it's like you're there. You're fifty feet tall and your nerves are made of gold. It's like you and the world are going exactly the same speed." (83, 84)"

Time and again, we witness the importance of pop culture for Marjorie, which she uses as a kind of (meta)language and source of analogies for making sense of her own experiences. With reference to one of Stephen King's novels, for example, she states that "school . . . wasn't like *Carrie* at all" (15). When she has sex for the first time with her friend Monty during a showing of *Halloween* (1978) at the drive-in, the real and the fictional worlds collapse in Marjorie's optics: "Above me, upside down, Jamie Lee Curtis was riding through a graveyard with this other girl, getting stoned. Monty stopped all of a sudden and let out a hot breath right in my face and fell on top of me like he'd been stabbed" (57). Monty will be the first in a series of boyfriends who do not particularly impress her before she meets Lamont, with whom she shares "the best time of [her] life" (73). Again she falls back on pop culture as a reference point when she compares their relationship to that of the lead characters in *Bonnie and Clyde* (10). "Good times. We were both working and Lamont bought that Hemi Roadrunner. We used to cruise Sooner from the big Mach 6 down around the Whataburger, just snuggling up on that bench seat with the Ramones grinding out a wall of sound, jumbo cherry slushes in the cup holders. You could start there and show how much we were in love and how normal we were and then how everything went wrong. That's what I'd do" (9). Another implicit filmic intertext, as will become obvious, is the Hollywood film *Natural Born Killers* (1994).

Toward the end of the novel, Marjorie also muses about the actors she would like to see cast in a film version of her memoirs and opts for Keanu Reeves as Lamont (211). Throughout the text, Marjorie supplies advice of this kind to "Stephen King" and admonishes her interviewer to "try to be nice to [her]" and to "tell a good story" (212). This metafictional commentary has several functions. First, it shows Marjorie's investment in the dramaturgy of the narrative of her life. In the end, that's all she has: her story; that is, the story of her crime is her legacy and cultural capital. Second, her comments, rendered as oral discourse, create the impression that she was actually having a conversation, implying that there is someone on whom her story could have a meaningful impact right when she is telling it. Yet, no matter how enthralling her tale, she is not Scheherazade in the *Arabian Nights:* there is no cliffhanger at the end of her narrative to guarantee her survival until the next day—there will be no new installment. Third, her comments also keep the reader aware of the futility of Marjorie's narrative: regardless of how engrossing and suspenseful her account may at times be, we are time and again reminded that we already know the ending. She does not plead insanity ("I consider myself sane. So does the State of Oklahoma. It's the only thing we agree on"; 32), and her last attempt at parole is denied, as she learns from Mr. Jeffries, her lawyer. In that sense, the reader has to accept the finality of Marjorie's execution: the novel literally ends with Marjorie's death.

In Marjorie's recounting of her relationship with Lamont, domestic bliss is soon lacerated by escalating drug abuse and incidents of domestic violence, which Marjorie plays down—she hits back, too—even if at one point their altercations end with Lamont being arrested. Marjorie's pregnancy leads to a temporary drug-free respite, and she and Lamont get married; yet after the baby, Gainey, is born, Marjorie relapses into her old habits of excessive drug and alcohol consumption. Her first prison sentence (for drug possession) is six months in the Clara Waters Community Correction Center—not "really a jail" (109) but a converted motel still equipped with the old furniture. It is during her first stint in prison that she meets Natalie Kramer, with whom she becomes sexually involved. Natalie will eventually move in with her and Lamont, and she and Marjorie continue, behind Lamont's back, to have sex involving all kinds of toys and gadgets that Natalie brings to their intimacy. However, Natalie will eventually become Marjorie's nemesis.

The prominence of the car and car culture in the novel and Marjorie's attraction to it anticipate the final road trip Marjorie and her family, including Natalie, will take. The road trip formula—the backbone of "fiction and nonfiction books by Americans who travel by car throughout the country either on a quest or simply to get away"—clearly is the generic basis of O'Nan's *The Speed Queen*.[5] In the context of the spatial turn in literary and cultural studies, the genre of the road narrative along with the "open-road" quest have been revisited by numerous scholars who have, among other things, pointed out its indebtedness to the western script (the horse becomes the car, so to speak[6]), its often overtly false romanticization of nature and Native American culture, and its gender bias.[7] In view of the genre's properties, it appears almost counterintuitive that a male author would invent a female protagonist to go "on the road," in a genre "traditionally focused, almost exclusively, on men and the absence of women."[8] That O'Nan has done so speaks for the author's disregard of literary as well as social conventions. Ruth Mayer places the novel in critical distance to "1990s highway killer movies" and to the "earlier road narrative and its celebration of rebellion," of which *Easy Rider* (1969) is a prime example.[9] By contrast, O'Nan stretches and reworks the formula, and his main character seems to exist only within the confines of the generic formulas she knows and tries to inhabit. The narrative picks up speed, literally, as the events unfold: Marjorie realizes that Natalie is also having an affair with Lamont. Even worse, their apartment is vandalized, the large amount of money they had borrowed to buy drugs is stolen (possibly by Natalie), and Lamont is badly injured by the money lenders, who cut off one of his toes. It is at this point in the narrative that things get out of control. They leave in a hurry, and the remaining plot unfolds as a road narrative and a killing spree that leads to the deaths of eight people, Lamont included. On the run from the money lenders and, later, from the police, Marjorie suggests they hide in the house she grew up in. The Closes, a middle-aged couple currently living there, are pressured into letting them stay with them: Lamont, Natalie, Marjorie, and Gainey (156). Lamont forces Mr. Close to withdraw money for the cash-strapped fugitives. At this point, with their backs to the wall, they have no inhibitions about using violence. And yet it is in the middle of Lamont having a violent outburst at the Closes' house that the narrative veers into the territory of melodrama, when Marjorie suddenly feels the urge to tell Lamont that she still loves him regardless of what happened between him and Natalie (or her and Natalie, for that matter): "In this gruesome scene, the reference is not to the well-known genre of splatter movies but to a soap opera-style relationship drama . . . keeping reality at bay."[10] In staging Marjorie's soap-operatic love confession parallel to the brutal murder of the Closes, the novel has genres grate against each other in a way that, for the reader, results in quasi-Brechtian defamiliarization (165–66). This is echoed diegetically by Marjorie also having her cultural scripts mixed up in a manner that demonstrates how pop culture no longer provides useful blueprints for her life experiences (if it ever did). In the end, "Lamont killed the Closes, if you want to get technical about it. He burned them alive" (164). Their body count increases further during a robbery (168) and later when Lamont shoots a police officer (197). On drugs and with Gainey in the backseat, Marjorie drives for several days through Oklahoma, Texas, and New Mexico. On the way, Lamont dies of injuries, and Marjorie attempts to kill Natalie (who survives and, later, also writes a book). In another meta-comment on the taken-for-grantedness of the ideology of frontierism and westward expansion implied in many road narratives, the novel has her wonder in response to an inquiry: "Why did we go west? I don't know. It was never a question" (189). It is at the Navajo Shiprock in New Mexico, where she intends to bury Lamont, that the police finally apprehend her. Later, on death row, one of Marjorie's favorite books, next to the Bible, is the *Discover America!* road atlas (30).

Stewart O'Nan himself has pointed to the fantasy work of the road trip in the American cultural imaginary:

> This is the American fantasy of getting into a bigass muscle car, getting completely fucked up on drugs, having great sex, killing a bunch of people, driving west into the night as fast as you can. We've seen that story so many times that we almost buy into the idea that it might be a fun thing to do. It's just a desire, an appetite, running unchecked, which is what the culture asks us to do. At the same time, we know it's the worst thing in the world for us . . . but it's fun, too! Although this is a satire of tabloid culture, and I do poke very pointed fun at it, it's not like we aren't all implicated in it. We all love—or I love, anyway—fast food. I love fast cars. I love taking drugs, getting drunk, having great sex. It's fun. So I don't bring the hammer down all the way.[11]

On the heels of films such as *True Romance* (1993) and *Natural Born Killers* (1994), *The Speed Queen* offers another variation of "aestheticized road rage" in a semi-ironic or double-voiced mode.[12] Marjorie appears to be doing many things at the same time: narrating the story, offering a projection screen, and inhabiting the cliché of the outlaw figure in American culture that continues to engage countless readers. Her life story merges with and becomes meaningful through iconic examples of popular fiction and film.

However, other genres and literary traditions come to mind as well: *The Speed Queen* can also be placed in the hard-boiled and noir traditions. One of its epigraphs is taken from the 1943 novel *Double Indemnity* by James M. Cain (the 1944 film version is based on a screenplay by Raymond Chandler). It certainly has elements of the crime stories of the pulp literature variety (incidentally, Quentin Tarantino, another auteur heavily influenced by genre fiction, was interested in the film rights to the novel[13]). To complicate things further, the narrative formula harkens all the way back to an even earlier form of writing—the gallows broadside, one of the first popular genres that shared stories of crime with a wider audience and has existed since the Middle Ages.[14] In colonial America, it was used by the Puritan authorities as a means of deterrence. In these broadsides, the culprit confesses to his crimes prior to his execution; in O'Nan's novel, there is no explicit discussion of Marjorie's execution (it is all procedural: she recounts the methods of execution in different states of the United States), yet a diachronic perspective going all the way back to the Middle Ages does suggest that there might be something archaic, perhaps even anachronistic about the death penalty itself. With Marjorie as its first-person narrator, the novel uses the generic convention of the confessional mode as well as the conversion formula—after all, she embraces her own religious conversion several times. To demonstrate her purification/reformation, she even quotes from the Bible and receives spiritual care by a nun. Marjorie's religious conversion is a narrative twist that strains suspension of disbelief. And *The Speed Queen* is surely not a confessional tale in the Augustinian tradition: Marjorie's tone is both self-conscious and shameless. Her confessor, in the dramaturgy of the novel, is neither God nor priest; ironically, it is Stephen King (as imagined by her). Thus, her confession certainly is somewhat unconventional: Marjorie does not display repentance, and she does not seek forgiveness. And there is yet another twist to it: even though "King" is the only addressee of her musings, Marjorie intends for him to eventually share her story with a mass audience. The tape recordings supposedly made of the story she tells also provide a structure for the novel: "Side A" (1), "Side B" (75) and "Tape 2 Side A" (143) are the section titles that encompass the novel's 114 chapters. Apparently the contract she has with "Stephen King" gives him the rights to "everything. My whole life really, that's what you paid for, isn't it?" (9).

The title of the novel has multiple layers of meaning: First, it refers to the drug colloquially referred to as "speed" that is used (along with a variety of other substances) by the protagonist. Second, it refers to her love of driving fast; the very first time she drives Lamont's car, she is pulled over by the police for speeding. She muses: "That was my nickname in the papers—the Speed Queen. I've always moved a little faster than the rest of the world. That's why I'm here, I guess. I don't always stop to think, I just want to go" (7). It also refers, third, to a key childhood story she relates, about racing down a hill on a tricycle, breaking her wrist in the process, when she is four years old. Unfazed, she goes right back to it after the fracture has healed (11–12), which foreshadows a pattern of self-destruction that will determine her life trajectory. Fourth, "Speed Queen" is, as one of Marjorie's fellow inmates brings to her attention, also a brand name of washing machines (191); thus, in the end, the novel even in part ironizes Marjorie's epithet by rather unglamorously associating it with a domestic appliance.

O'Nan considers *The Speed Queen* above all an American book, and he embraces its cultural specificity regarding the pop and the pulp it offers: "This is our culture. This is it. We're not making a lot of world-class ballet here, okay? Our composers are Chuck Berry and Michael Stipe. *The Speed Queen* is like my other two books in that it's unashamedly and unapologetic American in its concerns. It's supposed to be a carnival ride. It's fun, scary, and thrilling, then you get off and say, 'Whew! That was fast. Let's do it again.'"[15] In that sense, the book may be considered as and consumed like a "trip" on many levels. The epigraph taken from Golden Earring's classic song "Radar Love" (the band is not American, it is Dutch) certainly anticipates the novel's feverish quality and Marjorie's longing for fateful romance on the road (she certainly does have a soft spot for outlaw couples). In the end, having literally and metaphorically lost her moral compass, she admits: "I didn't know what I was doing. Just driving" (207). Narrating a road trip from a prison cell constitutes as big of a tension in terms of mobility and immobility as possible and effectually stresses the urgency of her storytelling as well as the way in which road narratives are not simply about mobility but about "imagining, recreating, and interrogating the term and terms of mobility."[16] As Ronald Primeau points out: "protagonists take to the road for a variety of reasons, and when goals are often frustrated, the irresolution makes telling the story more urgent."[17] The urgency of Marjorie's storytelling can hardly be exceeded. Ultimately, the novel contains Marjorie's outlaw mobility within the walls of a prison.

Published, like all of O'Nan's novels, to critical acclaim, *The Speed Queen* was in 2006 also adapted as a one-woman-play by Anne Stockton (starring as Marjorie) and director Austin Pendleton; it played at the Midtown International Theater Festival in New York City, where it won in the category of Outstanding Performance in a Solo Show, at Carnegie Theater, at the New Jersey

Repertory Company, and at Pittsburgh's Off the Wall Productions.[18] In an email correspondence, Anne Stockton described to me the times that she gave readings of *The Speed Queen* play and performed it to inmate audiences and staff in actual prison settings at Rikers Island, Sing Sing prison, Bedford Hills Correctional facility, and Beacon Correctional Facility between 2004 and 2010. Stockton visited both minimum- and maximum-security facilities and played female and male audiences, each time between thirty and fifty people. Above all, she remembers the responsiveness of her audience, along with bouts of restlessness and agitation during the parts of the performance that dealt with Marjorie's crimes. Stockton recalls women inmates, whom she (or the director) talked to after the play, identifying with Marjorie's fate, stating that "love got [them] in trouble too," "that they were in jail 'because of a man too,'" and that Marjorie "should have left Lamont" but that she also was "scary."[19]

O'Nan's response to the play was favorable and wary at the same time: "It's strange for any writer to come face-to-face with one of his or her characters. In the case of Anne Stockton's Marjorie, for me it's both satisfying and frightening. I'm happy she's captured Marjorie's innocence and insanity, but I also worry about anyone who hangs out with Marjorie too long."[20]

A review of the play after its opening in New York theaters draws comparisons to the play *Karla,* a 2005 death-row drama by Steve Earle based on the execution of Karla Faye Tucker, who in 1998 was the first woman to be executed in Texas since the Civil War, and to Tim Robbins's 2002 dramatic adaptation of the nonfiction *Dead Man Walking* (1993) by Sister Helen Prejean.[21] Unlike these texts, *The Speed Queen* is neither based on a true story nor overtly concerned with sentencing and death penalty reforms. O'Nan's novel, rather, is a satirical tale about all-American fantasies of freedom and their nexus with media consumption, violence (on-screen and off), and celebrity culture.

THE INS AND OUTS of prison also inform the second novel by Stewart O'Nan discussed in this chapter. In the much slower-paced novel *The Good Wife,* the protagonist, Patty Dickerson, is about to have her first baby when her husband, Tommy, is caught in a burglary that accidentally leads to the death of an elderly woman at the hands of Gary, his accomplice and the instigator of the crime. Gary blames the homicide on Tommy, who cannot prove his innocence and is sentenced to twenty-five years to life in prison for felony murder. Patty's life becomes divided between work, raising their son, Casey, and visiting Tommy in the various facilities he serves his sentence in. The novel is not characterized by the drama and heroics of crime fiction proper and even less by the spectacular, violence-driven action of *The Speed Queen,* even as Patty's life changes drastically while "the rest of the world is still there" (138); rather, the narrative focuses on how she doggedly manages her duties as "the good wife" after her husband's incarceration.

The 312 pages of the novel are structured into Stewart O'Nan's hallmark vignette-style chapters, which range in length from half a page to a little over ten pages and are organized into four main parts: "Arrested," "A Fair and Speedy Trial," "25 to Life," and "Conditions of Parole." These rather dry titles—suggesting impartiality, justice, and due process—are preceded by epigraphs taken from Fleetwood Mac song lyrics (mostly from the 1977 album *Rumors*), which creates ironic tension (and once more demonstrates O'Nan's familiarity with pop culture). It is this album, as O'Nan notes in the interview in this volume (see the appendix), that Patty would have enjoyed listening to on the radio as it was played endlessly. The brevity of the narrative sequences adds to the slice-of-life approach of the text (in contradistinction to more stylized plot constructions). While several pages are dedicated to Patty worrying about the outcome of the trial, the actual verdict (confirming her worst fears) is conveyed in merely half a sentence. The plot mostly proceeds in a straightforward fashion; there are no spectacular twists and turns, which, the novel suggests, is a good thing, as any such twist would in all likelihood be a turn for the worse. Readers are kept in suspense by continuously learning of more things that *might* go wrong, particularly after Tommy is wrongfully sentenced as the perpetrator of the homicide. The future seems to be full of potentially unpleasant surprises. And Patty "knows from experience that anything can happen" (308).

The Good Wife is written in the present tense and creates a narrative situation in which time moves slowly, monotonously, and yet relentlessly; the stalling of the plot dramatizes the long periods of waiting that Patty has to endure, the tediousness of bureaucratic procedures, and the difficulty to move on, to make things happen, to assert agency. With the exception of the first chapter, which cuts back and forth between Patty spending the evening in bed reading, waiting for her husband to come home, and Tommy and Gary's break-in, the third-person narration uses Patty as the sole focalizer, limiting itself to her point of view and conveying only what she knows, feels, and thinks. From her perspective, time clearly does not fly: "In waiting, time is slow and thick."[22] *The Good Wife* is in many ways a novel about the passing of time; similar to *Songs for the Missing, The Good Wife* valorizes waiting as an activity of its own and with its own quality, rhythm, and merits. Of course, Patty is not at all inactive or idle: she has a job (in fact, many different jobs over the course of the novel), she raises a child, and she takes care of her family inside and outside of prison while she awaits Tommy's release and their reunion as a couple and a family: "And they *are* a family. Patty's not about to give that up now, when they're almost together again" (214). The day of their reunion is the focal point of her life, which she dreams and daydreams about (158).

The first one hundred pages of the novel offer us insights into a judiciary and penal system that is overburdened, biased, and arbitrary. As Tommy cannot afford a lawyer, he is appointed a public defense attorney. Patty is worried: "The first time she meets their lawyer she wishes she'd tried harder to come up with the money. He's young and looks nervous in his skinny tie, a college kid dressed for an interview" (43). Tommy becomes the prime target of the prosecution after Gary cuts a deal with the prosecutor (97). After Tommy is sentenced (110) and his appeal is rejected ("the whole thing only takes fifteen minutes"; 160), his incarceration becomes a fact—of Patty's life, too. She regularly visits, later organizes their participation in the family reunion program (214), and works toward his parole, which is first denied (274) but eventually granted (279).

Patty, who married Tommy against the wishes of her mother, is protective of him and gets constantly defensive about their relationship. Yet, in his absence, she has to move back in with her mother, who helps her take care of her son, Casey. Apart from long periods of waiting, Patty's life as a stigmatized outsider in a small-town community is structured by work and domestic routines interspersed by a passing infatuation with a man (a friend of a friend), the celebration of family birthdays, and her sister's wedding. Contrary to what one may assume, following Patty's everyday life is not boring at all but makes for fascinating reading. In the process, the reader also learns all about the administrative and bureaucratic details of the U.S. penal system, with its occasionally abusive and discriminatory practices. Even as O'Nan's novel does not capture life behind bars, the novel engages in much detail with the prison as an institution with its own peculiar bureaucratic order, rules, and regulations. *The Good Wife* is a prison novel with a twist in the sense that it highlights the quotidian life of a person who is "doing time on the outside," to use a phrase Laura Fishman employs in the subtitle of her book, which describes the lives of women whose partners are inmates.[23] As the wife of a prison inmate, Patty is subjected to being strip-searched arbitrarily, having privileges (such as visits) granted or denied at random, and being kept in the dark about her husband's transfer to a different facility in a different part of the country. Every little detail or formality can matter in a bureaucracy that is regularly opaque in its functioning and erratic in its application of rules. Once, Patty brings photographs for Tommy but "the guards won't let her bring them in unless they're wrapped like a package" (139). When she brings them wrapped the next time, the package is torn up by the guards because "inmates are only allowed a total of ten photographs in their cell at any time" (139). Visits are sometimes also simply cancelled without any explanation.

The prison rules become Patty's rules, as well: "INAPPROPRIATE BEHAVIOR MAY RESULT IN TERMINATION OF THE VISIT. A sheet of instructions goes on to list conduct that won't be tolerated, including 'foul language,' 'outbursts of temper,' 'prolonged embracing,' and 'straddling-type contact.' The dress code is all about sex" (125). On another sign it says: "CHILDREN MUST BE KEPT UNDER CONTROL AT ALL TIMES" (126).

Tommy describes prison as "boring. It's like the army. You have to do whatever they tell you" (133). To Patty, the prison looks "like her old high school" (127). For her, prison is an institution that makes people virtually disappear: "It's as if he died, as if he never existed" (140). Her mother recalls her own experience of having been separated from her husband: "'It's like when your father was in the war,' her mother says. 'I'd get a letter, but he wasn't allowed to say where he was. I swear, sometimes it looked like swiss cheese.'" (117). Comparing her father's war experience with Tommy's prison experience might seem provocative, as it equates serving in the military—usually considered a patriotic duty—with serving time for having committed a crime. Yet the analogy speaks fittingly to the conditions under which the women live without their men. Much later, Tommy will find that the patients at a hospital they both work at remind him of "lifers" in "the way their rooms are set up like cells" (299). Prison, school, the hospital, the military: these institutions represent what Louis Althusser has called the "Ideological/Repressive State Apparatus" because they guard and constantly reproduce the social, political, and economic order.[24] Patty's comments on the analogies and similarities between various disciplinary institutions in modern society that on the surface seem to fulfill very different functions echo Foucault's studies on institutions as powerful forms of social control, most prominently the prison (*Discipline and Punish,* 1975) and hospital (*The Birth of the Clinic,* 1963). In the novel these institutions are not portrayed as inherently repressive in a more strictly Althusserian or Foucauldian vein, and the reasons for their existence are not explicitly called into question, yet it is in the details of Tommy's (and Patty's) ordeals that systemic injustices become evident. For instance, would Tommy have received a milder sentence if his lawyer had been more experienced?—not to mention the fact that Tommy has been wrongfully convicted in the first place.

Tommy's prison life remains largely unknown to us because the extent to which we share in it is limited to accompanying Patty (with Casey) on her visits. The novel does, however, occasionally hint at the violence of life in prison; one day Tommy is in the hospital due to "a little accident in the kitchen" (237). When Patty asks him how he managed to get cuts on his lower back working in the kitchen, Tommy dodges her question. Patty never learns what exactly happened, yet it seems more likely that Tommy's injuries were the result of an attack by a fellow inmate rather than an accident.

Punishment by incarceration, with Foucault, is "the most hidden part of the penal process"; "the criminal . . . is detached from society, he leaves it."[25] Patty notices that the prison Tommy is incarcerated in does not even appear on any map, "as if it doesn't exist" (241). Recently, cultural productions from Paul Scheuring's *Prison Break* (2005–9, 2017) to Piper Kerman's *Orange Is the New Black* (2013–19) have focused on the inside of the prison as a distinct microcosm. O'Nan's novel, in contrast, is more interested in showing that the prison system not only affects prisoners but also has a large impact on those on the outside who, although not sentenced, have their lives transformed in similarly adverse ways nonetheless.

In literary and cultural studies, the obvious genderedness of discourses of waiting has been addressed in some detail. It seems that in many contexts waiting is coded as a feminine activity: the good wife is the wife who waits. And yet, Patty is not Penelope—probably the most famous waiting wife of all—anticipating the return of an adventurous and victorious hero. Her husband is not a decorated veteran returning home from war—roughly, the modern equivalent to Penelope's Ulysses—but an inmate in a maximum-security prison. He does not elevate her social status but, to the contrary, presents a stigma she must bear in the small community she lives in with her mother and son, like a modern-day Hester Prynne. Still, the gender politics in the novel merit closer inspection. In the beginning of the novel, Patty is characterized as a woman who conforms to patriarchal expectations and looks to her husband in many matters, as the title itself already suggests. In the process of handling Tommy's case and being left behind/outside, it appears that she rises to the occasion even "without Tommy there to ask" (46). Although she often feels overwhelmed—"there's so much she doesn't know" (47)—she manages to work her way through the system and at times even work it to her advantage. How, in the pre-internet era, do you find the telephone number of the county jail when it is not in the blue pages? How do you acquire a public defense lawyer? How do you apply for welfare after finding out that you have been eligible for years? Patty does learn about the ins and outs of the criminal justice system, even if often the hard way, providing the reader with a glimpse of the bureaucratic maze that needs to be navigated by the many people who are in a similar situation. Still, she also continuously defines herself in rather stereotypical ways. For instance, she anticipates her age will negatively affect her marriage at the time of her husband's release: "She is twenty-seven, meaning she'll be fifty-two by the time he gets out—*if* he makes parole on the first try. There's no time off for good behavior like in other states. Her mother's only fifty-one, and look at her. Patty can't imagine him wanting that" (113). Patty questions her own desirability twenty-five years in the future but hardly takes into account that Tommy will then be twenty-five years older too. In another instance, when she and Casey are visiting Tommy through the family reunion program, she is happy to play house, prepare food, and generally perform a separate-spheres gender role. What she misses the most during her regular visits is "the privacy of their FRP, the luxury of whispering in bed, cooking for him" (247). She is also conflict averse and prone to pretending normalcy: "She lies to him. Every time she talks to him, she notices things she says. . . . More often, she lies by not telling him things. . . . Meanwhile she's lying to everyone else" (179–80). After starting a new job with more responsibility, she admits—if only to herself—that "she likes being a supervisor" (266). Certainly, Patty is in no way growing out of or away from her relationship with Tommy, but their involuntary separation still leads to her becoming more autonomous and self-confident.

Gender politics also involve the issue of intimacy, another topic the novel explores. Patty learns, in the absence of her imprisoned husband, to live with the paradox of having no intimacy in a relationship that is by definition characterized by romance—western marriage. The role of relationship-affirming rituals becomes crucially important for Patty's circumscribed interactions with Tommy. Every visit is carefully planned, including the clothes she picks for herself and her son to wear and what outside news she decides to tell Tommy about or conceal from him. Sociological scholarship has found that women whose husbands, fiancés, or boyfriends are incarcerated attempt to involve their loved one in personal and family life by relocating various everyday activities into the prison visiting room. As kinship gatherings, family celebrations, and romance are conducted behind bars, the prison becomes "Papa's house," an alternative site for the performance of "private" behavior.[26] Indeed, Casey only knows his father from visits to the prison and is uneasy around him, and Patty is bothered by, again in sociological terms, "the paradoxical 'institutionalization' of their own family life" and "the reach and intensity of the transformative effects of the carceral apparatus"[27]: "For Patty, that's the mystery at the heart of visitation. The way the system's set up, it's like a price they're supposed to pay over and over until they give up and stop loving the people they've come to see, and stop coming. That's why she has to submit, why, even as she hates everything about this place, she needs to be here" (217).

Casey grows up in a household with his mother and grandmother, the latter of whom also does much of the care work. The novel follows Casey from infancy to his teenage years. Patty worries about his reclusiveness and quietness, his aloofness toward his father, his difficulty in making friends, his refusal to wear glasses despite his nearsightedness, his affinity to fast food and chocolates. She tries to share some of her concerns with Tommy, yet at the time of his father's release from prison, Casey has long graduated and moved away, returning to his childhood home only for visits. Patty's initial sense that "the three of them need to get through this together" (125) seems disproven, and Patty—after fretting over her son for so many years—is glad that Casey is making a career for himself. When Tommy is finally released from prison after twenty-eight years, Patty experiences a sense of relief, if not exactly happiness. After his long absence, Tommy appears alternately like a child himself and like a man from a different time and place: "He's never used an ATM before, or a beeper, or a cellphone" (294). Even as Patty tries to help him adjust in many ways, it is unclear whether they will "find a new way to be with each other" (302). Tommy soon quits the job Patty was able to secure for him at her workplace; unsurprisingly, Tommy has difficulty reintegrating after spending almost three decades behind bars. His "good wife" remains unflaggingly optimistic. The novel ends with the following three sentences: "It's over. He's home. They made it" (308).

In the context of critical prison studies, *The Good Wife* is a valuable work that chronicles the everyday life of the wife of an inmate, which even under the best of circumstances is challenging and full of obstacles. Patty Dickerson is a literary heroine of a kind that cannot often be found. The novel creates a literary presence and visibility of the kind of "buried life" that has been at the center of American slice-of-life narratives since Sherwood Anderson first introduced it in his 1919 short story cycle *Winesburg, Ohio*.[28] *The Good Wife* once again confirms O'Nan's mastery in capturing the quotidian and rendering it in gripping prose.

BOTH NOVELS, *The Speed Queen* and *The Good Wife,* address the prison experience from different angles. They do not aim at a critique of the U.S. prison system per se—O'Nan is certainly not a political protest writer—and yet both, through their detailed presentation of Marjorie's and Patty's experiences with the often absurd and nonsensical, arbitrary, and contingent workings of the carceral institution, make visible the prison system's cruelty and potentially dehumanizing effect. Both novels are timely in the context of newly invigorated discussions about the death penalty and overall strategies of decarceration that are of concern to all Americans, not only to those in prison.

CHAPTER 5

Social Realism and the Myth of the Middle Class

Last Night at the Lobster and *The Odds*

All of Stewart O'Nan's novels emphasize the relevance of the material world, which in a late-capitalist setting usually is structured by practices, means, and spaces of consumption (malls, supermarkets, hotels, restaurants): goods sold or bought, services rendered or received. Regardless of any specific class status that may define the range of choices available in consumer capitalism, consumption is taken for granted as an activity in O'Nan's oeuvre. What is not taken for granted, however, are the repeated systemic failures people experience and suffer from within this system in the form of low-paid jobs, unemployment, or, more specifically, middle-class precarity after the financial crisis of 2007–8.

The topic of economic precariousness in O'Nan's works can be encountered most prominently and most explicitly in two of his shorter novels, *Last Night at the Lobster* (2007) and *The Odds* (2012). Both novels address the vulnerability of people who erroneously consider themselves safe from the turmoil of (stock) markets and labor retrenchments in an economic system that has moved from state-based to global finance capitalism or "neocapitalism," which is even more prone to crisis and is invested in the maximizing of profits rather than in the well-being of the labor force creating those profits.[1] The dwindling of the middle class, consisting of both blue- and white-collar workers, has become the object of much concern and critical attention. Scholars from various disciplines have drawn attention to the new forms of "precarious labor" that, under the guise of flexibility, have led to increased economic insecurity among lower- and middle-class workers and further hollowed out the idea that a good work ethic will lead to economic success and personal fulfillment, let alone the promise of the American dream: "Precarious labor does not only refer to the threat of unemployment, nor does it only cover conditions of work that are insufficient to secure the good life. Instead, the idea of precarious labor signals workers whose relationship to the social, whose very being, is contingent or at risk."[2] This risk is actualized in *Last Night at the Lobster*—"last night" here refers not to a preceding night but to the final night before the restaurant is shut down by headquarters. The novel covers a day in December, the last workday before Christmas, at a branch of the seafood chain Red Lobster in New Britain, Connecticut. It is the last time that the restaurant situated next to a mall will open its doors for customers. Its impeccable manager, Manny DeLeon, will be transferred to another restaurant chain branch under the same corporate ownership (and will be demoted in the process), together with a few of his employees. The rest of them will lose their jobs. Clearly, the setting of the about-to-be-closed-down restaurant is not particularly cheerful, which is reflected in the novel's rather melancholic and resigned tone. The novel apparently is a fictional, social realist dramatization of the kind of working conditions Barbara Ehrenreich and others have discussed in their studies on low- or minimum-wage labor in the service sector, which Ehrenreich, in particular, has encountered herself as an undercover investigative journalist for her book *Nickel & Dimed* (2001). O'Nan's novel zooms in on one such scenario of service labor and the bleak prospects it engenders.

As the novel opens, it is heavily snowing outside with a blizzard on its way, while inside the employees of the Red Lobster gather and get down to work on this last day of operation. Whether Manny's staff will appear or fail to appear for their shifts to him resembles a "test of loyalty" (13); many employees indeed do not show, "a nightmare" (21) for Manny, who tries to carry on as if the day was business as usual. He maintains his attitude of "lead[ing] by example" (8, 82) and sticks to his checklist of daily tasks. To the reader, Manny's work ethic may appear ridiculous in the face of the kind of misrecognition he experiences himself, and yet he never questions it himself, stolidly doing his duty of supervising his (reduced) staff and serving his customers. Reviews of the novel have commented in various ways on Manny's apparently misguided loyalty and discipline: "Manny's misplaced affection for Red Lobster is not risible, but tragic"[3]—tragic in the sense that it exemplifies false consciousness, workers' alienation and "other-directedness."[4] Conversely, another reviewer comments on the beauty rather than the tragedy of the novel: "*Last Night at the Lobster* makes beautiful sense in the span of O'Nan's writing life: It's a Zen koan of a book—Manny's life in all its integrity echoing out across a wintry mall in a Rust Belt American town."[5] Either way you look at it, the book addresses the futility of Manny's dedication and of the labor he relentlessly provides; perhaps the reader can think of him as a kind of fast food restaurant Sisyphus. This futility, however, does not diminish Manny's display of self-discipline, hard work, and moral idealism as core American values in almost Franklinesque fashion. With a nod to the protagonist, perhaps, Stephen King has called the novel "a book that embodies what's best in us" (book cover). In response to King's observation, another reviewer compares the setup of the novel to that of a book by Stephen King himself and finds striking similarities, even if in *Lobster,* obviously, neither zombies nor demons ever show up.[6] Instead the novel meticulously chronicles a day in the life of its characters without ever exposing them to ridicule or condescension. Manny lacks an explanation for the company's decision to close his branch: its revenue has not noticeably declined over the past year, and he has always complied with headquarters' guidelines—to no avail. Because Manny is unaware that parent companies frequently sell off assets simply to increase shareholder value and he has some difficulty accepting that the employees are treated as pawns, to him the decision made in a distant boardroom appears random and comes unexpectedly: "The thing is, there was no warning" (7). Manny tries not to feel guilty toward his staff, but he cannot help it and continually worries about the futures of his employees, individuals whose idiosyncrasies he has come to like or at least tolerate. Although he is in no way responsible for their firings, he tries to compensate for their abandonment by the company by helping everyone as much as he can: "Two months ago Manny had forty-four people working for him, twenty of them full-time. Tonight when he locks the doors, all but five will lose their jobs, and one of those five—unfairly, he thinks, since he was their leader—will be himself. Monday the survivors will start at the Olive Garden in Bristol, another fifteen minutes' commute, but better than what's waiting for Jacquie and the rest of them. He's spent the last few weeks polishing letters of recommendation, trying to come up with nice things to say—not hard in some cases, nearly impossible in others" (3).

The very notion of "survivors" conjures up the social Darwinist socioeconomic framework of late capitalism with its ideologeme of the survival of the fittest (those who do not "survive" are of course expected to take care of themselves and find themselves another temporary, low-paying job in the ever-shrinking job market). Manny still takes pride in "his" restaurant (despite the fact that he himself is viewed as entirely expendable by his employers) and cares for the people under his supervision—it pains him to see them being thrown out. Apparently, for him, the Red Lobster is more than just a place of work; much of his social life takes place there as well. He is still attracted to Jacquie, who is among those employees of the Red Lobster who will be out of a job at the end of the day. Even as his girlfriend Deena is pregnant and wants to marry him, his workplace romance with Jacquie still lingers in his thoughts and in his feelings, and he obviously has no qualms about it. Somewhat irrationally, he admits, he thinks he can still turn their affair into a lifelong commitment. On the last night at the Lobster he has to accept that this is not going to happen. His last conversation with Jacquie is sad, their good-bye final. Manny tells her: "You made me feel lucky" (143). Not coincidentally, his love for Jacquie corresponds to his attachment to the restaurant: Jacquie leaves him for good, and the restaurant is closed for good—"one begins to suspect that the main object of Manny's unrequited devotion is not Jacquie, but the restaurant itself"[7]—or, at least, that both are seriously intertwined.

Next to Jacquie, his team (or, perhaps, even "family") at the Red Lobster consists of Ty, the cook; the kitchen helpers, among them Fredo (who will eventually walk off after willfully damaging Ty's and Mannie's jackets and cars), Rich, Leron, Dom, and Eddie, with his "thick Medicare glasses" (9); and the waitresses Roz, Kendra, and Nicolette. It is these ten people who will work that very last shift with him. They embody a workforce that continues to serve customers until the very end according to the work procedures and routines painstakingly prescribed by the corporation that has sacked them.

Manny not only feels very responsible for his staff but also for his customers. Take, for instance, Mr. Kashynski, a regular at the Red Lobster who is "Manny's old gym teacher and coach from high school" (27); he and Manny often talked sports when he patronized the restaurant. When Manny tells him that the Lobster will close and that he will work at a new place, all Mr. Kashynski worries about are his coupons now being worthless, but Manny assures him that the Olive Garden will accept them as well. When Mr. Kashynski leaves, Manny runs after him into the snowstorm to exchange last pleasantries and to reassure him of his service: "Outside, in the snow, Mr. K. looks back and waves a last time. Manny waves and then watches him shuffle to his car the way he would his own abuelito, hoping all the while that he put down enough ice melter" (45). Manny treats Mr. Kashynski as a customer, with the utmost courtesy and respect—like he would his own grandfather, a kind of false intimacy perhaps. Again, as with Jacquie, the line between workplace sociality and private social relations is blurred, and the reader is made to wonder about Manny's "true" familial ties. Substituting work-based relations with staff and customers for private social relations, Manny is reluctant or unable to commit to relationships outside the restaurant—even with his pregnant girlfriend Deena.

Next to Mr. K.'s visit, the novel captures in much detail the interactions with two groups of customers during the lunch shift. First, there is a large group of customers who did not make reservations ("It's an office party, always demanding, and messy, and at the end they're likely to pool their dollars and scrimp on the tip"; 34), which has the waitresses struggle to keep up with their orders. As the group of fourteen celebrates the farewell party of a coworker (speeches and funny presents included), drinks and food are hectically provided. This scenario is another case of sociability in which workplace-based, corporate/contractual relations are reconfigured along the lines of private relations. Several scholars have analyzed such practices and their representation in popular culture through which working hours and work relationships are extended into previously private spaces and leisure time under the pretense of "fun." Ritualized after-work leisure activities (such as drinking at bars) date back to the beginning of corporate culture in America but have taken on a new dynamic under neoliberal governance principles.[8] In O'Nan's novel, the office party presents another instance of deterritorializing—that is, reaching out beyond the workspace and its work relationships—that mirrors Manny's dilemma in yet another way. This may be seen as one more effect of the all-encompassing force of neoliberalism. The second group of customers the novel focuses on during the lunch hour are two women, one with a child, who turn out to be demanding and annoying customers—the child creates a mess with his food and drink and, in the end, throws up on the restaurant carpet. To top it off, the mother complains about the service; not even venting to her waitress's manager—that is, to Manny—calms her down: "Manny's tempted—as he's never been before—to tell her her kid's a brat and that she's a terrible mother, and a terrible human being, but instead he gives her the contact info for the regional director and apologizes just to get her out the door" (61–62). The indignity of having to serve with a smile even the most misbehaved of toddlers (and his obnoxious mother) starkly demonstrates the hierarchy between food service labor and the customer. Manny faintly protests to the insolent customer but represses his impulse to stand up to her. When the company party at the other table finally leaves, thanking him for getting a table without a reservation, Manny subserviently replies: "Not a problem. Thanks for thinking of Red Lobster" (63) and immediately starts to muse about the phrase: "By now he says this as a reflex, but what does it mean? Who, besides the people who actually work here, thinks about Red Lobster? And even they don't really think about it" (63). This is one of very few fleeting moments in which Manny comes at least close to questioning the corporate identity pitched by the restaurant chain and his own incorporation of and adherence to it. Nevertheless, it is safe to assume that Manny will transfer quietly to the Olive Garden. O'Nan's novel, by making Manny the focalizer of events, subtly captures his complicity with a corporate logic and identity he is unable to dissociate himself from.

Only once during the course of the novel does Manny leave the restaurant to go to the nearby mall in order to get a Christmas present for his girlfriend Deena, whom he has been keeping at arm's length even though she is pregnant: "His mission is simple: Buy something she will love, and love him for buying" (73)—a notion that reveals his materialist mindset. Discarding all practical options, he turns to jewelry and buys diamond earrings. During his visit to the mall, he is distracted by his thoughts of Jacquie, who (like Deena) was pregnant from him but chose not to have the baby and even laughed at him when he proposed to her. Manny had also bought jewelry at the mall for Jacquie (a gift she will return to him at the end of the day), and he would still rather be buying a present for her instead of Deena. "Sometimes it's not the thought that counts, just the present" (78): Manny attempts to convince and at the same time to exonerate himself by inverting the well-known phrase.

Two epigraphs initially set the tone for the book. The first one consists of lines from Mexican American poet Luis Alberto Urrea's poem "Hymn to Vatos Who Will Never Be in a Poem." The second, in marked contrast, is the estimation of profits for Darden Restaurants, Inc. in 2005, which were expected to grow from 22 percent to 27 percent, as reported by msn.com. Red Lobster was part of the "Darden family of restaurants."[9] The bottom-up perspective of the poem commenting on the (metaphorical) invisibility of the "*vatos*" (guys) and their lives and the top-down perspective of the news item, and by extension the human interest of literature and the materialist interest of economy, are in marked tension with each other. This tension anticipates the skewed perspective that the characters in *Last Night at the Lobster* are exposed to as part of an expendable workforce whose labor, and thus livelihoods, are being totally subordinated to the increase of profits. Manny clearly is one of these "*vatos*." Of Manny's life, the reader learns that his *abuela* (grandmother), with whom he has lived, had recently died (97–98), that he has few memories of his mother (34), and that he recalls "early mornings delivering the *Herald* with his father and then later by himself" (6). The latter already anticipates the conflation of shared private moments (between father and son) with work (delivering the paper).

The 146 pages of the novel fall into five chapters: "Hours of Operation" (Manny arrives at the restaurant and prepares for the day's work), "Which Nobody Can Deny" (the restaurant opens and does lunch business), "The Most Wonderful Time" (Manny spends his break Christmas shopping at the mall), "Please Wait to Be Seated" (by far the longest of the chapters, describing business into the evening hours), and "End of Day" (Manny closes the restaurant for the last time). The setting of the novel has been compared by reviewers to the kind of *tableaux vivants* found in the paintings of Edward Hopper: "Who knew an all-you-can-eat shrimp buffet could evoke such mournful, Edward Hopper-ish pathos?"[10] Minna Proctor observes that "O'Nan has a penchant for characters who recall figures in Diane Arbus photos—wide-eyed and gimpy, dreary and pathological; seductive in a roadkill kind of way. Manny is no exception. He's propelled forward by virtue of momentum, his underlying passivity less biochemical than the upshot of having been beaten to a pulp by life. It is, sadly, rather too easy to dismiss him—and, even more sadly, something of a challenge to slog through this short book."[11]

Even more than a visual culture of marginality and isolation, the novel evokes notions of the performative and the theatrical due to its depiction of ritualized service labor routines, its scripted and rehearsed dramaturgy and speech acts, and the stage-like quality of the restaurant space. When Manny arrives at the restaurant and prepares for the day, he is setting the stage for his customers, so to speak, while the readers are also allowed access to those spaces that for the customers are behind-the-scenes: the workspace, the kitchen, and the storage room. At the same time, from another vantage point, Manny is also part of the setup. In explicit and implicit ways, Manny performs and negotiates his social interactions upfront and in the back as manager, waiter, ex-lover, and so on, and he at times confuses professional and personal roles. Following Manny and his staff through their last day at the restaurant, the reader witnesses the succession of customers and the staff–customer encounters that bespeak the repetitiveness of service labor and its seriality along with the necessity for the staff to routinely perform in certain ways. As to the mode of representation, O'Nan's slice-of-life realism (or, more precisely, "slice-of working-class life" realism[12]) maintains the reality effect in no uncertain terms. Like *The Good Wife,* the novel is told in the present tense, conveying a sense of stalling, paralysis, and lack of agency. The third-person narration adheres to Manny's limited point of view, which heightens the effect. The novel is about the tragedy of missed opportunities and unrealized attraction. Manny's mantra, "there's still tonight" (41), is an illusion that carries him through this last day at the Red Lobster but does not lead to a happy ending.

O'Nan's novels often are tied to special days in the American civil religious calendar, holidays that have a special meaning for Americans individually and collectively, reminding them of their "imagined community" through shared festivities and rituals of consumption on these occasions.[13] In *Last Night at the Lobster* the upcoming event is Christmas. It may be considered a heartless irony that the restaurant is closed in the prime season of shopping and consumption. The Christmas idyll and its connotations, in any case, are thoroughly deconstructed. The snow, rather than conveying a festive spirit, is a cause of concern to Manny, who worries about its removal. As the snowfall continues, Manny becomes absorbed with this task: "O'Nan's comprehensive approach can evoke the tedium of the job too effectively—five full pages describe how Manny uses a snowblower to clear the restaurant's path. But his vivid portrait of the Lobster ultimately conveys, somewhat miraculously, the warmth and comfort the restaurant provides Manny."[14] Eventually the snowstorm causes a temporary power failure, and the restaurant has a blackout, forcing customers to eat by candlelight. A couple Manny goes out of his way to accommodate remains reserved despite his best efforts; after their "candlelight dinner," they even try to get a discount on their tab. Business in general is slow. Manny at last has a funny rather than annoying encounter with a busload of Chinese tourists escorted to the Red Lobster by police; the tourists have fallen sick and need to use the restrooms. Seeing the bus, there is a spike in excitement ("We got a bus"; 123), which quickly dissipates with the realization that the bus's occupants are not customers but people in need of a restroom and a glass of water. Manny is happy to provide both; still, this anticlimactic turn encapsulates in a nutshell once again Manny's frustrated expectations of doing business on the last night of the Lobster.

As there are no customers to attend to, Manny and his staff share something of a "last supper," a drink, and old stories: "Inside, everyone has gathered around a low table in the bar, as if the night is over. Rich and Leron lounge in soft chairs with their feet up, still wearing their aprons. Manny and Jacquie split, out of habit taking seats on opposite sides of the group. Roz has her shoes off and is telling about the time Fat Kathy's ex-boyfriend got arrested for fighting with her in the parking lot" (116). While sharing stories about former employees, Manny muses that "it seems they're talking about a whole other place" (118), and "he can't figure out how they got from there to here" (119). Manny's sense of nostalgia is intensified by the sharing of these stories and memories, yet he cannot reconnect. After he hands out lottery tickets to his remaining staff members along with a drink as a "Christmas bonus" (135), they watch the winning numbers being drawn on television—unsurprisingly, none of them win. The dream of a big win, which could solve all economic problems just like in "The Star Money" fairy tale, is the topic of the other novel dealt with in this chapter.

Throughout the novel, situations are shown that speak to the marketization of social relations and private intimacy and vice versa. At the same time, O'Nan's social realist novel is not primarily concerned with exposing and denouncing this dynamic but rather with paying respect to people like Manny who, with the utmost care, do their work and expend all their energy into relations that are far from reciprocal by a long shot. In that sense, the book serves as a reminder for the reader to not take such labor for granted but to show some respect for those who render it.

STEWART O'NAN has described *The Odds* as "a kind of companion piece" to *Last Night at the Lobster.*[15] In it, he further explores the theme of downward mobility experienced by America's middle-class, specifically on the heels of the 2007–8 financial crisis. The novel narrates how this crisis bears upon Art and Marion Fowler, a middle-aged Cleveland couple faced by both economic and emotional bankruptcy, so to speak: private bankruptcy and the breakup of their marriage of almost thirty years. They have lost everything: both are unemployed, their house is about to be foreclosed on, and their relationship is in tatters; whereas Marion has had an intimate relationship with her lesbian coworker Karen (unbeknownst to her husband, yet "an empty secret"; 141), Art had a whirlwind affair with a younger woman, Wendy Daigle, whom he intended to leave his wife for. Even though Art's affair did not last and he returned to Marion, she is still unforgiving, resentful, and hurt. In this private "state of exception," Art and Marion come up with a plan that under regular circumstances would be entirely out of character for both of them: they spend some of their last resources on a package trip to Niagara Falls, their honeymoon destination of many years ago, in order to gamble at one of the casinos there and go for broke.

Their trip to the much-sugar-coated Niagara Falls ("that fabled and overwrought cauldron of new beginnings, away from any domestic, everyday claims"; 1) is a desperate measure: they hope to win big. They travel with a bag full of cash (all they have left) across the border into Canada (unusually enough, by bus, not car, as part of their cheap package deal). In need of nothing less than a "miracle" (3), they intend to bet their money at the casino. But first they treat themselves to some luxury at the hotel, where they have a suite with a view of the falls. To all outward appearances, they seem like regular tourists reminiscing about their honeymoon many years ago or renewing their wedding vow rather than an estranged couple with nothing left to lose.

While the 179-page novel spans their trip to Niagara over the Valentine's Day weekend of 2010, flashbacks recount how Art and Marion ended up in such desperate circumstances: how they believed in the mantra of upward mobility and bought a house that "was out of their range" (70); how they took on a mortgage they technically were not qualified for; how they got cheap loans for house renovations and repairs, temporarily—or so it seemed—solving "a simple liquidity problem" (71); how they both unexpectedly lost their jobs; and how it all turned into a life-shattering financial disaster: "The crash was too fast, or he was too slow" (72), in Art's perspective. Now, enjoying perhaps their last vacation before they have to declare bankruptcy, they are alternately tense and joking about their misery. Niagara Falls, it appears, is a good place to escape reality and forget about your sorrows, as Art notes: "This is Niagara Falls, nothing's real here" (28).

The setting of the novel is somewhat overdetermined, as it showcases the utter "commodification of romance" by a culture industry producing and catering to romantic expectations at the falls—a place that refers to itself as the "honeymoon capital of the world"—through ubiquitous offers that play on the wedding theme in an atmosphere of perpetual candlelight and kitsch amid a spectacular natural setting that is commonly, as Eva Illouz explains, "endowed with a quality of the sublime, namely, an association with the ineffable and pure intensity of feeling."[16] As such, it also caters to what in the novel is described as a "sweet, false nostalgia" (130) in an attempt to simulate a romantic fulfillment that must remain utterly utopian. On the occasion the novel covers, Valentine's Day weekend, this fabricated sense of festiveness drawing on a manufactured spiritus loci is especially palpable: there are couples in high spirits everywhere, many of whom appear almost beside themselves with joy over their weddings and honeymoons. Art and Marion's weekend trip also includes conventional touristic experiences—from the horse buggy ride to the restaurant with a view—which they partially enjoy along the lines of the dominant "structures of feeling" visiting couples are interpellated by and they partially reject as hokey.[17] Their experience of married life seems to have proven many of the fantasies and expectations offered for consumption at Niagara Falls wrong. But even as they see through the false romance of the place, they are still in part awkwardly relying on it to unfold its magic.

Yet Niagara Falls as a destination is not only about romance but also about adventure, both literal (as in the spectacular stories of people having gone over the falls) and metaphorical (as in the casino "adventures" that make the Canadian side of the falls a special attraction). As the author notes: "I wanted Art and Marion to work out their private feelings in a public space, and one most people know. Niagara Falls is a fantasyland, both natural and artificial, beautiful and ugly, American and Canadian. We associate it with corny, old-time romance but also with risk and danger, so it seemed like a perfect stage for a pair of reluctant daredevils."[18] Niagara Falls as a stage, of course, also conjures up Hollywood classics and stardom—along with instances of love gone wrong and betrayal—as in the famous film with Marilyn Monroe and Joseph Cotton that bears the name of the place: *Niagara* (1953).

The larger themes of this novel and "love story" (its subtitle) are intimacy, loyalty, (in)fidelity, and the possibility of a second chance. In that sense, the story of Art and Marion also evokes Stanley Cavell's well-known interpretation of what he refers to as the "Hollywood comedy of remarriage," a popular cultural script that allows couples to negotiate their relationship on equal terms beneath all of the genre's in-your-face innuendo and slapstick humor and to overcome their alienation from each other.[19] In the films Cavell discusses, the time before remarriage presents, for him, a time of not only crisis but also reflection on individual and shared orientations and life choices, entailing the promise of a more egalitarian bond and projecting remarriage as a second chance for both partners, who—now more self-reliant—no longer need or use each other for purely conventional reasons. In line with generic conventions, partners will at the end usually have transcended those, enabling them to share truly mature love and affection for each other. Even as Cavell's Emersonian reading of Hollywood comedies has been criticized as somewhat overbearing, the thrust of his argument pertains in crucial ways to the situation of the couple in *The Odds*.[20]

Similar to the characters in the films Cavell discusses, Marion and Art take their trip together as if it were the last thing they would do as a couple. A very real crisis and the prospect of a new beginning are offered to us here too. Clearly—and for added drama—they have very different views on their joint project. Throughout the novel Art and Marion examine their lives, mostly separately, in interior monologues. They negotiate their status as a couple, observing and scrutinizing each other's actions. Even as they are in this together, their discrepant attitudes and divergent perspectives on their relationship and their future together (or apart) become obvious. Art wants to rekindle their marriage as if this really were "a second honeymoon" (6; he has even bought a ring for Marion and anticipates erotic encounters in their hotel suite, an expectation that will not be met at first); Marion, on the other hand, is still angry at him (30), harboring and constantly expressing resentment, and is largely indifferent if not opposed to the continuation of their marriage. She even looks forward to living alone, imagining life as a single in an apartment of her own. In that sense, their common project at the falls may also turn out to be a temporary suspension of their eventual separation, a predivorce outing, as it were.

Their discrepancies in perspective are evident on many levels: on their first night at their hotel, Marion gets sick after dinner and spends the rest of the evening miserable in the bathroom. Art, by contrast, fondly reminisces about his hotel stays with Wendy, rich with champagne and sex. Having sex the next morning with Marion, Art feels "rewarded," is "pleased enough with his performance," and feels confirmed in his belief to "keep trying" (49), while Marion is regretful and feels she is sending the wrong message ("Making love was a way of laying claim to each other, both of them openly agreeing to renew that bond"; 49). And she muses: "He was playful after they made love, frisky, yet she felt no residual giddiness, no surge of energy, only fatigue and a vague bitterness" (51). The contrast between their explicit exchanges and what remains unsaid could not be starker.

Throughout, the narrative ponders the question of intimacy and familiarity in the Fowlers' long-term relationship. Marion's chronic inscrutability (as perceived by Art) and Art's repetitive and predictable responses and neediness (as perceived by Marion) constitute the conditions under which they can or cannot stay together. A well-rehearsed choreography, a pas de deux of attraction and rejection and of mixed messages characterize Marion and Art's interaction. Art's rehearsed attempts at romance, in another instance, with a red rose (65), champagne, and a ring, conflict with Marion's half-hearted resistance to his advances; this repeatedly leads to misunderstandings, even in their declaration of love for each other (159–60). While Art believes that his overt gestures of romance and performances of intimacy via well-established cultural symbols and practices might actually rekindle their love for each other, Marion considers these rituals to be in glaring contradiction to Art's past behavior as an adulterous husband; hence, she finds him hypocritical and feels the urge to reject and punish him. As readers, we take turns sharing the perspective of both, and we may wonder about their future together. Will they have a second chance at their marriage? Can they bury the old suspicions and wounds and change the(ir) script? How does the romantic atmosphere at the falls impact or frame their interaction? Shifting from existential questions hovering over them to mundane ones, such as how to divide their household items (beds, for instance; 60) in case of divorce or choosing their next activity at the falls (buggy ride, birds conservatory), the novel switches between varying levels of intensity (and, at times, superficiality) quite superbly. Art observes: "At home they would have never picked apart their lives so clinically, airing their regrets as if they were some other couple's. Like middle age, vacation provided a necessary distance, an extra perspective" (92). Even Marion admits that "she was glad they came" (68) and thinks that "they made a good-looking couple" (154).

The theme of second chances, however, is neither limited nor primarily related to the novel's story of love lost (and perhaps re-found) but is first and foremost at the center of the other story arc the novel offers: Art and Marion's get-rich-quick scheme to solve their massive financial problems. Gambling is not only commonly associated with the novel's setting of Niagara Falls but also symbolizes a last-ditch effort to remedy a desperate situation. To the couple it seems that by gambling with the last of their cash, they are just doing what finance capitalism (incidentally also referred to as "casino capitalism") had been doing with their livelihoods all along but on a much grander scale. Art lost his job because the insurance company he had worked for his entire life was bought out. Similarly, Marion is let go after many years at the same company. In an interview, O'Nan describes both of his characters as "old-style workers" who started their work lives in a no longer existing economy of paternalistic capitalism and were "loyal to their companies thinking that the companies would also be loyal to them."[21] The novel's representation of employment quandaries echoes Richard Sennett's diagnosis that regimes of labor have become "erratic and discontinuous rather than routine and determinate."[22] In that sense, their financial disaster is systemic rather than self-induced. The novel presents gambling as a not-wholly-inadequate or counterintuitive response to their predicament, analogizing it to the mechanisms of financial capitalism, the economic system Art and Marion have fallen prey to.

The contingencies of their life choices, the futility of their plans due to the illusionary promises of upward mobility, are laid bare for Marion and Art as their lives have become dangerously precarious. Their story spells out the larger ramifications of what Sanford Schram calls "the return to ordinary capitalism" under the arc of a new "privatized Keynesianism" that "heightens the precarity of ordinary citizens" in a "new, more financialized economy that makes money for those at the top while everybody else is weighed down by multiplying forms of debt, whether in home mortgages, student loans, credit cards, or medical bills" and in which private citizens sustain the economy through their personal debt.[23] In the novel, Art calls playing along with this kind of pyramid scheme his "crooked bookkeeping" (77), continually raising the balances on their credit cards to make mortgage payments on time. Schram's diagnosis reveals the vulnerability of the middle class, among others, as a case induced by what Lauren Berlant has termed "cruel optimism"—that is, desiring a version of the good life that ultimately turns out to be harmful.[24] The Fowlers clearly have participated in the American economy exactly as intended by neoliberal wealth redistribution schemes and in the end find themselves at the casino, literalizing the precariousness of their financial circumstances.

The novel reflects this kind of precarity and insecurity on a formal level as well, emphasizing the dependency on chance that one has to cope with. The twenty-seven chapter titles suggestively play with probabilities of various kinds and reiterate the contingency of likelihoods under the conditions of late capitalism: "Odds of a U.S. tourist visiting Niagara Falls: 1 in 195"; "Odds of a vehicle searched by Canadian customs: 1 in 384"; "Odds of a married couple reaching their 25th anniversary: 1 in 6"; "Odds of getting sick on vacation: 1 in 9," and so on. These titles prepare us for the novel's finale at the roulette table in the casino. Putting two middle-aged American citizens in the gambling hall, playing to recoup their losses, may be an apt metaphor for a system that thrives on putting at existential risk its less privileged and thus expendable participants.

The discourse of miracles—be they romantic, sublime, or financial, or any combination of the above—illustrates the circumscribed agency of the protagonists who are at the mercy of powers beyond their control. Marion reads up on the "miracle at Niagara," which refers to a boy, Roger Woodward, who survived going over the falls without protection (the first person ever to have survived such a fall): "She imagined the boy . . . struggling to swim against the current. She thought she knew the dread and panic of being swept inexorably toward the edge, except that sometime in these past few months, whether to preserve her strength or her sanity, she'd stopped fighting. Now she was just floating, waiting to go over" (85).

Similarly, the Ripley's Believe It or Not! Museum (134), which Marion and Art visit, asks for a willingness to believe in its spectacular attractions, oddities, and sensations—and could be read as foreshadowing the fairy-tale ending of the novel. As we are nearing their fateful casino visit, the title of the novel (also reflected in the chapter headings) makes sense: "While they knew what was waiting for them, going from the artificial silence to the artificial din of the casino was like walking onto a factory floor. In vast, windowless rooms, row upon row of players sat tethered to plinking, flashing machines, impervious to the outside world. It might have been day or night, summer or winter. They might have been on Mars. All that mattered was the next bet, the next spin" (166).

The casino is described like a kind of factory space with the players as workers, busy at their machines in an artificial, windowless, and secluded environment. Art and Marion likewise set themselves to work and are about to place their bets. Art has read up on the Martingale method while Marion approaches the game more intuitively. Marion and Art, having been set up to fail in their everyday life, for once are able to beat the odds stacked against them. After a few twists and turns, they win big. The novel closes: "'We won!' he cried, hugging her. 'We won!' she cried, hugging him. But of course, they'd already won" (179).

The ending can be interpreted in at least two different ways. First, it is a happy ending in no uncertain terms, leaving lucky Marion and Art at the roulette table enjoying their miracle win, suggesting that they made it, and that they will also make it as a couple. The very last sentence seems to imply this. In that sense, the novel's two plot arcs converge: the marriage (and infidelity) plot, on the one hand, and the downward mobility/second-chances plot, on the other. The last chapter is titled "Odds of a divorced couple remarrying: 1 in 20.480," once more evoking Cavell's remarriage argument, even if not in literal terms. Second, the ending can be read as a cathartic moment of relief from their existential worries that does not necessarily imply Art and Marion's romantic reunion, which may rather be projected into it by readerly expectations. Yet, even as the reader may wonder about Art and Marion's future together, we are invited to share their joy and relief on this one night, in which they have, for once, beaten the odds. Third, of course, is the chance that they play on, as do so many one-time winners, and lose all in the end.

In one of the reviews of *Last Night at the Lobster,* Nathaniel Rich writes: "He [O'Nan] is a poet of strip mall ennui, road rage, fluorescent lighting and the sparse lawns of prefabricated real estate developments. His characters strive to make their mortgage payments, hold full-time jobs and keep the refrigerator stocked, but struggle to fend off the lurking nightmares of domestic crime, alcoholism and war trauma. They buy lottery tickets, and they always lose."[25]

In a sense, then, *The Odds* delivers what *Last Night at the Lobster* did not. Whereas Manny DeLeon succeeded neither at rekindling his affair with Jacquie nor at saving the restaurant nor at winning the lottery, Art and Marion Fowler's story has a different outcome with its surprise, fairy-tale ending, at least if we take it at face value. Manny's regret of missed opportunities and his longing for a second chance with Jacquie and for the Lobster are squashed; at the end of *The Odds,* a second chance for Marion and Art, contrary to much of the evidence ("You couldn't relive your life"; 98), is not foreclosed by the narrative. It is up to the reader to opt for reasonable likelihood or for unwarranted optimism, even as a social realist reading leaves little room for the latter.

CHAPTER 6

Habits of the Heart

Wish You Were Here; Emily, Alone; and *Henry, Himself*

Leo Tolstoy once famously wrote in the opening lines of *Anna Karenina* that "happy families are all alike, every unhappy family is unhappy in its own way." In the O'Nan universe, such a dramatic dichotomy (happy/unhappy) does not apply. O'Nan instead portrays his prototype of an American upper-middle-class family, the Maxwell family, as a microcosm of ordinary rather than extraordinary (un)happiness in three volumes of "family procedurals." The author shows the possibilities as well as the limits of intimacy in couple, parent–child, and sibling constellations and in how these relationships grow and change over time, how they mutually affect each other, and how care work and interfamilial jealousies and humiliations sit side by side.

The "habits of the heart" in the title of this chapter refer to those habits that Alexis de Tocqueville, as early as the 1830s, famously diagnosed as constituting the basic tenets of the American mentality and that Robert Bellah and his coauthors took up in their sociological study under the same name in the mid-1980s.[1] With Tocqueville, Bellah and colleagues identify the family as the foundational unit of American society and family values as core civic virtues. If the dominant ideology of Americanness is individualism, as they (and many others) suggest, then the looming question is what holds American society together in terms of community spirit. The family as "a system of inclusion" mitigates the capitalist ideology of market individualism in creating a protected private space of solidarity and a sense of community and belonging that is then extended to ever-larger realms of private and public civic culture:

neighborhood, church, town, state, nation.[2] As a microcosm of the communal, the family (and the nuclear family, in particular) is based on biological kinship and thus is concerned with lineage and bloodlines; since its invention in the nineteenth century, the bourgeois family has become the dominant form of social organization and as such has taken center stage in the American cultural imaginary and in American literature.[3]

The three novels considered in this chapter constitute a trilogy that tells the story of the Maxwell family across three generations. The first of these novels, *Wish You Were Here* (2002), has garnered much critical acclaim and has brought O'Nan to the attention of an ever-larger audience in the United States and abroad. Whereas *Emily, Alone* (2011) is a sequel to *Wish You Were Here,* the final work, *Henry, Himself* (2019), is a prequel to the preceding two novels. Both *Henry, Himself* and *Emily, Alone* are narrated from the point of view of their title characters; Henry's perspective nicely complements Emily's. In *Wish You Were Here,* no single point of view of a character is privileged. In fact, the novel's complexity is generated through the shifting of multiple narrative perspectives and how they play off against each other.

The different installments of this trilogy have been compared to various canonical American texts tracing the lives of family members through the late twentieth century, such as Joyce Carol Oates's *We Were the Mulvaneys* (1996), Jonathan Franzen's *The Corrections* (2001), and John Updike's Rabbit series (1960–2002). O'Nan's trilogy shares an interest in the state of the American family as the prime site of care and of dysfunction. Somewhat contrary to these works, however, O'Nan's trilogy about the American family is less concerned with spectacular crises and drama and pays less obvious attention to the political and social changes taking place around the Maxwells. Again, it is rather the implicit normativity of family routines and their effect on family members that interest O'Nan: how do individuals outgrow their familial origins, if they do, and how are they kept back, even stifled, by them? How can familial protocols and "feeling rules" that, according to Arlie Hochschild, "guide emotion work by establishing the sense of entitlement or obligation that governs emotional exchanges" be changed?[4] How do the formative years predetermine the range of choices in adult life? And how does the Maxwell family reflect class? In what follows, I discuss the three novels in the order of their publication.

Stewart O'Nan's eighth novel, *Wish You Were Here,* recounts a family reunion at the Maxwell summer house situated at Chautauqua Lake; this shared vacation follows a long family tradition but faces an uncertain future after the recent death of Henry Maxwell, the family patriarch, as his widow, Emily, plans to sell the cottage, which has been family property for generations. The Maxwell family consists of Emily, now the owner of the cottage, and her grown children, Margaret and Kenneth, who both have families of their own. Arlene, Emily's sister-in-law, joins her for the drive from Pittsburgh, where they both live, to the lake in upstate New York. Despite their differences, Emily and Arlene have become friends or at least companions in old age and are moving toward a more sisterly relationship and a "fragile agreement" (505) at the end of the novel. Margaret, mother of Sarah and Justin, is going through a divorce from Jeff and has a history of excessive drug use, alcoholism, and other forms of self-destructive behavior. While at the lake, she has to cope with the news that Jeff plans to remarry. Kenneth, a struggling photographer-artist, and his wife, Lise, are the parents of Sam and Ella. Both Margaret and Kenneth bring their own set of problems to chew on as they meet their mother and aunt on this family vacation, which, as it turns out, may be the last one in a long series. On the novel's first page Emily muses as she gets into Arlene's car: "It would be the last time she made the trip up, the last time she saw the cottage" (3). Thus, the beginning of the novel already foreshadows a sense of an ending. While accompanying the characters to the lake—Arlene and Emily from Pittsburgh, Kenneth and Lise with Ella and Sam from Boston, and Margaret with Sarah and Justin from Detroit—the reader anticipates that all of them will face fateful changes and turns during their week together.

Yet, instead of unfolding one central overarching plotline, the novel takes us through the days of the vacation one at a time, from Saturday to Saturday, in what Ruth Franklin describes as a "relaxed framework."[5] Each long chapter—Saturday (1–48), Sunday (49–135), Monday (139–198), Tuesday (199–290), Wednesday (291–350), Thursday (351–435), Friday (437–501), and Saturday again (503–end)—starts with breakfast and ends at night. The content could well be summarized by enumerating the family activities, which include the usual thrice-daily meals, swimming, a visit to a flea market and a bookstore, post-dinner video films, tennis, and golf. The highlight of their family vacation is a spontaneous trip to Niagara Falls, the place that defines "the standard of happiness" (315)—a site that O'Nan returns to in his novel *The Odds: A Love Story* (2012). Yet, the spectacle of the falls does little in the way of easing tensions but rather renders explicit and highly visible the different dispositions of the family members. As might be expected, consumer culture looms large in all their activities: at the falls, they take a boat trip and visit the restaurant with a view and, finally, a gift shop. The title of the novel, *Wish You Were Here,* references the tourist experience, as it is a typical phrase used on picture postcards; Kenneth, who still has artistic ambitions as a photographer, wonders whether being "unoriginal" and "incompetent" and producing work that was "secondhand" (484) means that he is only good enough for postcard photography: "Maybe that was his calling" (484). But the title not only indirectly refers to

Kenneth's thwarted or unrealized artistic ambitions; it also contrasts the real experiences during the family vacation with the cultural assumptions of idyllic holidays pointedly exemplified by Emily's writing a standardized and cliché postcard to her friend Louise back home in Pittsburgh, which she cannot seem to get mailed (229, 231, 353). Holidays may be replenishing. Family holidays hardly ever are and, as O'Nan shows us, can on the contrary be quite exhausting: in the novel, the holiday week is filled with quite a load of doubts, anxieties, and disappointments for every single character, and every family member is more or less successfully working through problems of his or her own. The little cottage with its "enforced intimacy" (293) is a place of wildly circulating and unfocused energies, good and bad, that can hardly be contained. Similarly, frequent rides in the car—yet another confined space—are characterized by moods and uneasy interactions. Yet the subtle manifestations of dissonance throughout the week never erupt into an open quarrel, nor do characters even so much as raise their voices at each other. The beauty of the lake, "the spell of Chautauqua" (89), seemingly compensates the vacationers for all the bottled-up tension and stress since restraint is one of their most cherished habits.

The novel is narrated in the third person, yet the narrator is not omniscient; rather, in a very egalitarian way, the points of view of all the novel's characters are used to tell the story, with narrative perspective changing with each new section. The chapters include on average twenty sections that are marked only by numbers; thus, it is up to the reader to look for clues as to whose perspective informs any given section. Even the family dog, Rufus, gets to be the focalizer of one short section (327–28)—after all, the book is dedicated to two dogs, as we can infer from the novel's dedication: "For Dewey and Diamond, our two Rufuses." Rufus will also continue to be a "character" in the two following books on the Maxwell family. As all the perspectives appear side by side and in their interplay come to shape the organic unity of the novel, the reader sees in the sum of the different points of view the dynamics of silence, misunderstanding, and indifference. It also becomes discernible that intimate thoughts and concerns are shared only selectively by the characters and how much each of them keeps to himself—or to herself—and how words, in those rare moments of sharing, may come out entirely in the wrong way or be voiced at the wrong moment. It is through the contrast and the tension between the dialogues (what is actually said) and the largely unspoken inner lives of the characters that the novel's captivating little dramas unfold and the manifestations of inner familial alterity are exposed. The various degrees of estrangement between partners and between children and their parents are not necessarily rendered problematic or even marked as pathological; rather, they are presented as part and parcel of the workings of the institution of the bourgeois family: as a close-knit web of intimate relations, it is organized around generational difference and power asymmetries and is thus by nature ambiguous. The characters become round characters for the reader through their contributions to conversations, through their inner reflection, and by what others think about them, with the difference between these modes of characterization also elucidating the kind of self-censorship they engage in.

The novel explores familial relationships along vertical as well as horizontal axes. Emily is growing into her new role as the family matriarch and in many ways considers herself superior to the others. Margaret makes fun of her new air of self-importance in a conversation with her brother: "He [Dad] made all their money, and now she's the big financial genius" (194). Still, Emily is the representative of the older generation and, quite simply, owns the house and is the host of the family gathering. She appears to be highly opinionated and (in the view of some family members, her sister-in-law included) lacks any sense of humor (186). She is still mourning the death of her husband and observes of herself that she has become "sentimental" and prone to crying. Emily's sentimentality again and again surfaces during (and is linked to) scenes of parting: even watching people say good-bye to each other on television reduces her to tears (9). This disposition for sentimentality is puzzling to family members as it contradicts their perception of her as, in fact, lacking empathy. In that sense, one may consider Emily's tears not so much as an expression of her general emotionality but rather as a quite specific and instinctive reaction to the loss of her husband. "At her age she was allowed to be sentimental" (167), Emily contends and links her tearfulness to her memories of Henry and their shared life. Yet her portrayal of Henry is rather sober and not overtly romantic: "Henry had been reliable to the end. . . . The only time Henry had surprised her was by dying, and she had not suddenly become a stronger person, just alone" (465). To contain and redirect her feelings, Emily resorts to formalities and to seemingly material matters. She wants all family members to make a "list" (202) of things they would like from the cottage before it is cleared and sold, and when there is a general lack of response (along with anger at the idea of selling the house), she takes offense at it and complains about everyone's disinterest. "Of course. She would be their past. Time was not a circle or a line but a kitchen, a lamp, an armchair" (145). For her, memories reside primarily in things. Emily's demanding attitude leads to regular disappointment in her children and grandchildren. For one thing, she is insensitive and feels entitled to any information regarding their lives, only to be annoyed when they are not forthcoming—Kenneth, for instance, cannot help but dodge her questions about his job situation, which she holds against him: "I deserve some explanation" (85). Her feelings toward her daughter, Margaret, are rather mixed and include guilt (109) but also anger and sadness. She sums up her daughter's situation quite drastically: "What a mess. It was not a judgment, just a statement of fact. A sadness. And probably, somehow, partly her fault. She was not blind" (109). Even while Emily continues to display an air of quiet disapproval toward her daughter, she will ultimately help Margaret financially. Clearly, monetary support is easier for Emily to give and for Margaret to receive than any kind of emotional support—let alone true empathizing at eye level.

Arlene, Henry's sister and Emily's sister-in-law, appears to be less worrisome and to have hardly any demons in the closet. She is much less normative in her view on family matters and is certainly little concerned with formalities and decorum. A former schoolteacher, she enjoys the company of books as much as that of her relatives, particularly that of the younger generation. She seems more introverted than her sister-in-law and is more of a participant-observer of the Maxwell family drama: she is somewhat of a confidante to Margaret, which Emily resents, but is not as openly critical of Emily as Margaret. Among Arlene's saddest memories that she revisits during the week at Chautauqua is her affair with the love of her life, Walter, a married family man whose teaching assistant she had been: "Their love had been improper" (339), and Walter eventually ended their affair, breaking her heart. Arlene had only confided about this relationship to Henry, who helped her get over it. She has remained unmarried: "Her life was her own, no one else's, and she had done the best she could" (90). For Arlene, Chautauqua is a place of "timelessness" (372). The cottage holds Arlene's childhood memories yet now is lawfully Emily's, but Arlene does not insist on custom: "She'd never said to Emily that the cottage wasn't hers to sell, that by rights it still belonged to the Maxwell family, of which she was the eldest living member, but she suspected Emily knew how she felt" (83). Neither of them raises the topic directly because, despite their differences, they are also companions sharing the same generational background and have known each other for a long time. At Chautauqua, they go out together, reminiscing over dinner and cocktails (244).

Both of Emily's children, Kenneth and Margaret, have clearly not fulfilled her expectations. The upward mobility taken for granted by Emily and Henry's generation has eluded Kenneth and Margaret, who in their early forties are still not fully financially independent. Margaret is repeatedly referred to as the "black sheep" of the family (160) and has been at odds with her mother as long as both can remember. With the character Margaret, the topic of changing gender roles is added to the subject of intergenerational strife. While Margaret recalls that her father used to take her side in arguments with her mother, she also remembers him as "a weak ally" (59) who would always, in the end, cave to her mother's wishes. Yet he never forgave her for calling him out on his spinelessness, "and the two of them [Henry and Margaret] were never the same, like Jeff after her rehab. She would never understand why men were so brittle. For all their posturing they didn't know how to fight, how to win or lose without letting it wreck them" (59). Unable or even unwilling to deal with their daughter and her rebelliousness, her parents had eventually sent her to a boarding school. Many years later, there is now an uneasy truce between her and her mother. After many wrong turns, Margaret now considers herself a survivor and after reading a Sue Grafton novel compares herself to its protagonist, Kinsey Millhone, a hard-boiled female detective (408), in an effort at symbolic empowerment. Her tone is markedly different from that of the other characters in the novel: abrupt, straightforward, harsh; still, she is a vulnerable person. On several occasions, she reflects on her present moment and on how she got there: "But she'd made it, here she was, living fucking proof. The fact made her laugh, made the simplest motion—reaching up and fitting these bowls into each other—solid and remarkable" (288). At the lake, she stays up late at night, talking to Ken or to Arlene, smoking various substances on the porch. Regarding her own chances at recovery and healing, she remains cautiously optimistic to the end: "The sun warmed the trees, left everything beneath them in deep shadow—a postcard. The parking lot was empty, only the flimsy railings leading to the snack bar, the old man in the ticket window reading his Stephen King. There was nothing to be afraid of. That life was behind her now—not gone, no, it was still a part of her, but it belonged to the past, and she needed to keep it there, to relinquish her grip on it, as hard as that might be, if not impossible" (463). The postcard analogy, here, is affirmative and points to something that is worth preserving, unlike in other scenes of the novel where postcards are used figuratively in different ways. The ironic juxtaposition of a man reading a horror novel and Margaret's insight that there was nothing for her to be afraid of emphasizes her newfound belief in her ability to keep her inner demons at bay.

Kenneth, to turn to the other grown Maxwell child, has always been devoted to his older sister and, apart from that, has tried to get along with everyone while finding time to follow his true calling: photography. It is Kenneth's perceived weakness—his career choices and "lack of ambition, his problems holding jobs" (85)—that have been cause for concern and disappointment to his mother. Kenneth is introverted; in this regard, he is more like his father and aunt than his mother. Obviously, he does not comply with contemporary models of normative maleness. Arlene, who is protective of him, observes that as a teacher, she "had seen a thousand oversensitive boys like him and was convinced that their desperate eagerness to please came not from a lack of confidence but from how much their parents needed them to succeed" (85). Often during the week Kenneth tries to get away from the family to take photographs, and he daydreams about authoring photo books on the "faded turn-of-the-century world of Chautauqua" (234)—an idea that, in fact, predates and anticipates the trend of ruin photography in American rust belt cities and towns. As a photographer and aesthete, he perceives of the world in terms of "shots" and "the next shot"; around family members, he is evasive and at times aloof, conflict-averse, and highly aware of the mutual dislike between his wife and his mother. When Emily asks him toward the end of the week, "Do you really think your photography is going to get you anywhere?," he finds her purposefully "cruel" (371). Like his father before him, he is caught amid cross-generational female rivalry between his mother, on the one hand, and his sister and his wife, on the other, "a female love of control, at once social and familial, the complicated opposite of the macho dream of independence, dominance through intimacy" (367–68). Now, after his father's death, he technically has moved up in the family hierarchy to the position of "man in the house." Yet he feels uncomfortable in that role and burdened with a "responsibility he didn't want" (471). Just once, "he put his father's cap on and sat up straight, peering over the windshield, swiveling his head to watch for oncoming traffic, as if he knew what he was doing" (473). In this scene, Kenneth conveys a sense of awkwardly mimicking a cultural script of manhood he is deeply at odds with. In fact, it might be true of all the characters of his generation in the novel that they struggle with trying to conform to (or renounce) socially prescribed and pre-scripted models bequeathed on (or forced upon) them by the "Greatest Generation" (Tom Brokaw's term in his classical study on the heroism of those who grew up during the Depression and then went on to serve in World War II—people such as Henry, the family patriarch).[6]

Kenneth's wife, Lise, who has been in a relationship with Kenneth for many years, is painfully aware of her continuing outsider status among the Maxwell clan and her utter powerlessness in that constellation. Lise regularly vents her jealousy ("She was just frustrated, having to compete with everyone for Ken"; 337) and complains about Emily ("everything's a crisis with her"; 28). She feels excluded and stressed: "This wasn't a vacation" (73). Still, for her, it's all about Kenneth: "She just wanted them to connect again" (147). She wants "just to be included, to not be forgotten" (207). Throughout the novel, she urges Ken to spend time with her, preferably alone. She wants to rekindle their romantic relationship while trying to be supportive of his ambitions as a photographer but has to spend most of her time and her energies taking care of the children and trying to get along with some family members—for example, Margaret, who "seemed strange to her, alien and almost comic in how completely she played the black sheep" (160)—while avoiding others whenever possible, especially Emily. She realizes that "Ken loved her in his own distracted way" (164). As she shares "his family's annual melodramas" (420), her neediness makes her vulnerable to feelings of rejection. In a conversation with Margaret, she illusionary asserts: "But the majority of people, I think you'd agree, are happy with their lives. Otherwise they'd change them" (163), to which Margaret replies that she was naïve in disregarding the manifold economic and social-familial pressures as well as the psychological deformations preventing such change.

All four of the children, Sarah, Ella, Sam, and Justin, experience their own anxieties but keep them from the adults and, in part, from each other. Sarah and Ella, two girls in the throes of puberty, are concerned with matters of sexuality and physical intimacy. Serious and intellectual Ella, in fact, develops a crush on her playfully flirtatious cousin, Sarah, and struggles to hide her infatuation. Sarah has a boyfriend, Mark, who is at a camp and is very slow to write; when she finally receives his letter, it is a breakup note. Sarah then seeks out other male attention, all the while using the dog, Rufus, as an excuse to get out of the house. In her mind, Sarah is imagining romance and sex. Somewhat in contrast to her outward demeanor, she had been taking care of her brother when her mother fell apart, and she seems to have inherited the kind of oppositional and rebellious defiance Margaret shows toward Emily. Ella, on her part, imagines intimacy with her cousin and wonders what it would be like to kiss her.

The two boys, Justin and Sam, seem to have little in common. Justin is a timid boy, afraid of his mother's harshness and temper—and of many, many other things. He misses his father and, like Sarah, would rather live with him than their mother. During his stay at the lake he grows a little more self-confident. When tubing on the lake under the guidance of Kenneth and Lise, he eventually overcomes his fear and enjoys the outing. Sam seems to be equally troubled. He practices his own kind of resistance and defiance by compulsively stealing from other family members and at the store and is almost caught in the act once, when he takes Sarah's watch. Both boys are very fond of their Game Boys and huge fans of the Pokémon game and thus are absorbed in a virtual world with its own language and imaginary the grown-ups do not understand.

Henry is the absent presence of the novel, the empty hub of the Maxwells' world, as it were, both in acknowledged and unacknowledged ways. He is mourned and missed, specifically by Emily and Arlene, and yet, due to his absence, the family is being reconfigured, with all members being assigned new roles. The family, even if less than picture-perfect and partially experienced as stifling, still is the prime site of identification and belonging for the Maxwells. No matter how conflict-ridden, it does provide ontological security for all its members, in both literal and symbolic ways. In the end, Emily will sell the lake cottage to pay for Margaret's mortgage and thus secure her daughter's post-divorce middle-class status and her grandchildren's educational opportunities. She does this out of a sense of familial duty toward her daughter (and a sense of guilt); to the shocked Arlene, she refers to it harshly as "clean[ing] up after her [Margaret's] mess—again" (246). Emily obviously finds no other way of expressing care than in materialist ways.

The atmosphere in the family may remind us of the gothic, specifically of the unhomely, but the gothic mode is used in this novel in a more general sense. One of its epigraphs is taken from Daphne du Maurier's gothic novel *Rebecca,* which famously begins: "Last night I dreamt I went to Manderley again." Certainly, the cottage on Chautauqua Lake does not equal the beautiful estate of Mr. de Winter in du Maurier's novel (there is perhaps a hint of irony in such a comparison); however, the specters of the past also surround the characters in O'Nan's novel in at times mysterious ways: memories of childhood, of marriage, and of love found and lost linger on. There is a sense of darkness and gloom inside the cottage permeating the bad-weather days, when Emily is contemplating old age, loss, and death. Less dramatic are aspects of the everyday gothic that the novel also presents us with. Early in their vacation week, Ken, returning from a flea market, stops at a gas station and, when going inside to pay, finds the place deserted. Eventually he leaves. Later on the Maxwells hear on the news that the gas station was robbed and the attendant, a girl, kidnapped. This apparently happened only minutes before Ken walked in. He is interviewed by the police and gives his eyewitness account. This "Mystery of the Gas Station" (110) or "the mystery of no one being at the gas station" (73), as the family begins to call it, remains enigmatic as the police cannot find the missing nineteen-year-old Tracy Ann Caler: "'Looks like whoever robbed the place took her with them . . . You think a place like this is safe, a little town like Mayville. It's not'" (127), a policeman tells Ken. Eventually the case becomes an FBI investigation, an unheard-of occurrence in the small town of Mayville. The girl's disappearance continues to occupy Kenneth and Emily; in particular, Emily becomes virtually obsessed by this case. Kenneth thinks about the girl as he drives around taking photographs, and he imagines finding her. However, the case is not resolved. The uncanny disappearance of Tracy Ann Caler occupies the minds of the Maxwells for various reasons, giving shape to their unspoken anxieties and providing a way to externalize them. Within O'Nan's oeuvre, of course, this episode echoes the inciting incident of his novel *Songs for the Missing,* where the teenaged Kim is abducted on her way to her job at the gas station.

Wish You Were Here certainly is Stewart O'Nan's opus magnum, not only because of its sheer size but rather because of its scope. The Maxwell family who, at least at first glance, almost seems to meet Rockwellian standards of the American family, as its members are white, Christian, and firmly upper-middle class, unravels in front of our eyes as unresolved conflicts come to the fore and color every interaction. The novel masterfully integrates the interplay of the characters' subjective narration with a formal sophistication in terms of structure and language. The text reveals its textual complexity, along with the complexity of its topic (family relations), through "the multiple and often conflicting meanings woven into it" that can be captured and made legible via "the linguistic devices of a new criticism-approach: paradox, irony, ambiguity, and tension";[7] these four different devices render the constellations in which the novel positions its characters in relation to each other and in the spatial and temporal setting of the holiday week at the lake against the backdrop of the book's postcard-cliché title.

Now, to come back to the beginning of this chapter, the novel does not portray the Maxwell family as particularly happy or unhappy but as average, albeit in complicated ways. The text ends on a mixed note of accomplishment, resignation, and reconciliation, and one character succinctly sums the vacation up: "It had been a full week" (494). And another: "Once again, they'd survived" (514). These kinds of calm, cool, and collected estimations indicate the "absence of melodrama" and of any overt form of sentimentalism in O'Nan's novel.[8] Given O'Nan's investment in creating round characters in this text, it is hardly surprising that characters from the novel also have "survived" the book in the sense that they have been revisited by the author—first Emily, then Henry—in subsequent books.

EMILY, ALONE (2011), which, when it came out, was lauded by the *New York Times* as "O'Nan's best novel yet," is a sequel to *Wish You Were Here* centering on the titular protagonist, Emily Maxwell, who at age eighty, now spends her time listening to classical music on the radio, running little errands, going to church, planning and receiving visits from her children and grandchildren, and recalling memories of the past.[9] In fact, the novel is "a moody, lightly comic and absolutely captivating rendering of that most un-sensational of subjects: widowhood and old age."[10] It is, one may want to add, a subject that seems to be more often glossed over in contemporary American literature than the topic of aging men and their legacy. Emily's closest companion is (still) her sister-in-law, Arlene, who seems more of a rebel: she still smokes and dyes her hair a striking red; she also lives by herself in a nearby neighborhood in Pittsburgh.

Emily is keenly aware of the changes in her surroundings—many of her neighbors have left or died and new ones have moved in. Most of her friends are gone, for that matter. Her friend Louise has passed and her friend Kay, too—without Emily even knowing. "Of the old crew, she [Emily] was the last, and once again she wondered where the years had gone, and why she was still alive" (187). Sharing some sort of common destiny, she and Arlene are united, hanging on, taking care of each other—even if they themselves would not put it quite this way. O'Nan has dedicated *Emily, Alone* to his "mother, who took me to the bookmobile," from which the reader may infer that the novel has autobiographical elements.

The epigraph, taken from Virginia Woolf's novel *To the Lighthouse* ("Could it be, even for elderly people, that this was life—startling, unexpected, unknown?"), sets the tone for this novel, in which Emily is still sorting out her life, quite literally at times. The challenge to accept old age permeates the book. The dedication and the epigraph, taken together, bestow on the novel also a commemorative function, a kind of symbolic immortalization of its protagonist—as the literary alter ego of the author's mother perhaps—following Woolf's novel, which similarly addresses the ways in which art (a portrait as an aesthetic act of memory) may prevail over death (of the person portrayed) according to the idea of art's immortality. *Emily, Alone* is narrated in fifty-five short chapters and vignettes, some as short as a couple of paragraphs ("Forgetfulness," 132) and others several pages long. The novel starts out with the longest chapter, the exposition titled "Two-for-One," which refers both to a breakfast buffet coupon as well as to Emily and Arlene's close relationship. The novel's structure is formally similar to that of *The Good Wife,* but whereas we follow the "good wife" Patty Dickerson for close to thirty years, we follow Emily only from late summer to the next summer; the book covers the family calendar and its civil religious holidays, which Emily anxiously awaits as opportunities to get together with (and to get annoyed by) her children and grandchildren once again. Sometimes these family meetings are more and sometimes less to Emily's satisfaction; it seems that these encounters are always lagging behind her expectations and that her wishful thinking and her longing for harmony perpetually clashes with the realities of family life. Still, these visits matter a lot to Emily, as they give meaning to her life; on the textual level, the holidays function as a basic structuring device. As the novel moves from Thanksgiving to Christmas to Easter and Mother's Day, it also covers such other events as the yearly flower exhibition, a visit to the art museum, eating out with Arlene, attending church, and cemetery visits. But this does not mean that the world at large is simply shut out of Emily's life: the year is 2008, and Emily somewhat reluctantly gives her vote to John McCain in the Republican presidential primary. Her granddaughter Sarah, Margaret's daughter, is working for the Obama campaign in Chicago. Both of Emily's children are Democrats, it turns out, whereas Emily has been a lifelong supporter of Republican presidential candidates and presidents, especially Bob Dole and the older Bush, "someone she could believe in" (205). The intergenerational quarrels within the Maxwell family we know from *Wish You Were Here* are thus expanded to include the grown-up grandchildren and their political positions.

The novel's opening begins to unfold a seemingly banal plot, yet it is powerfully evocative in many ways. The reader first (re-)encounters Emily and Arlene on their way to a restaurant: "Tuesdays, Emily Maxwell put what precious little remained of her life in God's and her sister-in-law Arlene's shaky hands and they drove together to Edgewood for Eat'n Park's two-for-one breakfast buffet" (1). Arlene's diminished navigational and coordinating skills as a driver appear to anticipate the overall fragility of their lives as every intersection and roundabout seems to pose a challenge. Emily is apprehensive as other drivers honk at Arlene for slowing down the flow of traffic. The short drive through the city has turned into a dramatic weekly adventure for both of them.

During this ride the reader also learns about the city of Pittsburgh, Emily's city, and about the changing fate and the decline of neighborhoods in the aftermath of deindustrialization. Clearly, the setting of Pittsburgh is both close at hand and very deliberately chosen—it is O'Nan's hometown and the favorite recurring setting of his texts. As his books frequently offer detailed descriptions of the city's history and geography in the vein of neorealism, he has been claimed as a Pittsburgh writer. Emily's familiarity with the city is not only geographical but also densely biographical: she came to Pittsburgh as a young woman and now, in old age, "each street was saturated with memory" (11). Yet Emily is also aware that the urban landscape has been shaped by conflicted histories of class and race: "As they neared East Liberty, block by block the houses deteriorated, porches sagging, windows boarded over, retaining walls spray-painted. Trash dotted the yards and sidewalks, and at every intersection huddled fairy rings of signs from last week's election, the winners and losers drenched alike by the rain" (7). In a more abstract way, the reader may be tempted to look upon Emily either as an allegorical embodiment of postindustrial decline and her old age as mirroring the aging of the place she lives in, an urban space in a late-capitalist consumer landscape battling decay, or as an allegory of the old social order with its classism and its futile resistance to change (selectively drawing on the example her namesake in William Faulkner's famous short story "A Rose for Emily" set up). Emily's having moved from small-town America to a city or, more precisely, to suburbia certainly makes her to a degree representative of her generation, but a purely allegorical reading would not do justice to her round character, even if the descriptions of the novel's protagonist and setting are suggestive of such an approach.

When, at the end of this first chapter, Arlene collapses at the breakfast buffet, "blood running from a cut above one eye," and an exasperated Emily shouts "For God's sake . . . somebody help us" (15), the vulnerability of both of them in their old age is sharply realized. Hence, the first chapter impressively establishes a sense of fragility, transitoriness, and ruin framing the characters and the setting (later Emily will explicitly refer to her own body as a "ruin" [208] that no one would want to see).

Because Arlene is hospitalized, Emily, who had relied on her husband and later on Arlene to drive her for most of her life, has to drive herself for the first time in many years to get around. After having tested her late husband's Oldsmobile, which turns out to be too big for her (the showy car is also vandalized in front of her house), she buys a smaller car for herself with "the largest check she'd ever written" (75), a Subaru, which she thinks might in fact outlive her. Of course, the novel is obviously not a road novel in the conventional sense, and we would have a hard time comparing it to *The Speed Queen;* still, it is a novel about the nexus of mobility and self-determination and presents the story of an old woman refamiliarizing herself with the skill of driving and getting back on the road, so to speak, if only to drive around the city to do her errands. For her, owning and driving her car is a matter of regained independence and autonomy. The car is both a vehicle and a catalyst of her late emancipation: "The novel, in a way, hinges on that car—a bright blue Subaru Outback that she (hilariously) worries is too flashy—which, both literally and metaphorically, allows her greater agency over her own life and, in the months that follow, sends her into something of an emotional tailspin."[11]

Yet, even if there is an emancipatory aspect to Emily's driving, it seems her major confinement is not so much one of (im)mobility but one of relentless adherence to etiquette: throughout the novel, she remains observant of bourgeois norms with a religious fervor. Hence, Emily's conservatism is not really due to a politically conscious self-positioning but rather reflects her enthusiastic and at best semiconscious adherence to bourgeois conventions and her slightly snobbish and highly opinionated outlook on the world. As is not uncommon with people who have achieved upward social mobility, her performance of upper-middle-class respectability may be a little overzealous. Her sister-in-law certainly thinks so. One reviewer refers to "the diligently achieved and now-fading upper-middle-class world of Emily Maxwell from Pittsburgh. Decades ago, Emily managed the class climb into the country club world of Pittsburgh by marrying Henry Maxwell."[12] In many ways *Emily, Alone* is as much about generation as it is about class, which are both defined by specific "habitus" (French sociologist Pierre Bourdieu's term[13]) and "taste cultures" (Herbert Gans, following Bourdieu[14]), two sociological concepts that can help shed light on Emily's character. Emily's habitus (her class-specific habits and dispositions acquired biographically) and her "taste" in music, the arts, and aesthetic pleasures in general align her with an "upper-middle" taste public and culture. Members of this taste group "want culture and want to be cultured," yet they prefer literature and art that is at best mildly experimental or abstract and that, in any case, has already broadly garnered symbolic capital.[15] According to Gans, this taste public prefers "symphonic and operative works of nineteenth-century composers" to "compositions of earlier centuries and contemporary music."[16] Emily's musical taste fits this description nicely. Her enthusiasm for paintings by Vincent van Gogh similarly echoes Bourdieu's famous use of French art to describe the way in which class-differentiated and habitus-based cultural competences can be identified and evaluated.[17] When Arlene and Emily visit the Art Institute's Vincent van Gogh exhibition, it is precisely a well-known painting of his sunflowers series—an example that, following Bourdieu, has often been used to differentiate taste cultures—that at first receives her special attention.[18] But aside from this thoroughly canonized painting that (according to Gans's classification) could also be enjoyed by the "lower-middle culture" for the sheer sake of its colorful flashiness and figural/topical accessibility and intelligibility, Emily especially enjoys *Bridge in the Rain,* a painting inspired by the Japanese artist Utagawa Hiroshige, which she counts among her personal favorites—and she holds back on a somewhat disparaging comment toward Arlene, who is exuberantly indulging in her own (and very different) aesthetic experience of the painting. Hence, Emily's cultural taste conforms to that of the upper-middle class, whose social status and prestige she has acquired through marriage in the same way as her cultural preferences. In other words, she has internalized a taste culture that she thinks of as her own—a misconception she shares with many, if not most, individuals. The museum visit, among other things, also constitutes a kind of "conspicuous consumption," a term Thorstein Veblen coined to describe the display of one's own (perceived) socioeconomic standing through the public consumption of (cultural) goods and services.[19]

Emily's acquired taste culture consists of a set of values that is not restricted to aesthetics but is all encompassing and obviously stands in stark contrast with the value system of the younger generations. Time and again she clashes with her children: "A child of the Depression and the Great War, raised in privation, Emily prizes thrift and industry. Her children—products of the 1960s and, of course, their parents' financial stability—prize self-expression over all."[20] The behavior of the next generation often strikes her as inappropriate, and she often perceives her children's neglect of formalities as deliberately intended to offend her. Often this antagonism plays out between herself and her daughter, Margaret, over the smallest of matters, for instance, the writing (or lack thereof) of Christmas thank-you cards; in Emily's view, "Margaret simply didn't care. Thank-you notes belonged to the same category of useless formalities her square parents followed blindly, like sitting down to meals at prescribed times or going to church on Sunday. People should give gifts because it made them happy" (129). Margaret's "ditzy hippie logic exhausted Emily" (129). Emily, on her part, is hung up on etiquette and is upset about Margaret's perceived rudeness over the course of an entire chapter ("Ingratitude"): "A thank-you note was so little to ask—the minimum, really" (130). When Margaret does write her "a full-fledged letter," Emily's anger is still unappeased, as she now finds Margaret's response exaggerated and suspects it has more to do with her "new ideals" of gratitude and positive thinking (as part of the AA twelve-step program) than with her, Emily, personally (130). This behavior smacks of "the pursuit of unhappiness," as Paul Watzlawick has so aptly described.[21] In her more self-reflective moments, Emily admits that she is hard to please, but this insight does not carry over. It is her estranged relationship to her daughter that Emily counts as one of the continuous sources of sadness and a reminder of personal failure in her life; yet she also sees it as a mirror of her own relationship with her mother and, hence, a well-deserved punishment. A compulsion to repeat seems to be at work within the family. She remembers well that she gave her mother much grief, which culminated in her leaving home; she never even went back for visits after she married Henry and moved to the city. In one of the last chapters of the book, Emily does drive to Kersey, her hometown, where she visits her parent's graves. It is a place she for years had been reluctant to visit, telling herself that she had outgrown it, but her reluctance was actually because of her unwillingness to be reminded of her own as well as her mother's regrets. She knows now that this visit could be her last chance, and she finally seeks closure with her past.

In revisiting her own daughter–mother relation, Emily attempts to come to terms not only with the strained relationship to her daughter but also with the thoroughly estranged relationship to her daughter-in-law, Lise, the daughter of an affluent family, who calls Emily out on her snobbish demeanor, which Emily resents (their thinly veiled mutual dislike also has a class-specific dimension). By now, though, they have learned to simply avoid each other.

Along with the theme of fragility introduced early on, the novel traces Emily's struggles for equanimity, which she attempts to achieve through idiosyncratic habits and routines whose well-structured monotony is designed to prevent unforeseen and unexpected events, which to her are almost always unpleasant and at times even disturbing. On the whole, her world becomes smaller, "narrowing down to this house, this room, this moment" (129). Her days are filled with small pleasures and small frustrations, a little bit of reminiscing and introspection, regret, some calmness, too: "There was nothing like crossing things off her list to raise her spirits and her sights" (243). Settling her affairs, both literally and metaphorically speaking, is her priority. Going over her last will with her daughter and her son is important to her, as is getting rid of clutter and useless possessions. When things do not go as planned, Emily becomes easily dejected. Small setbacks and misfortunes can cause "a feeling of pointlessness" (157), for instance, when she detects scratches on the door of her new car. Yet the question of what to keep and what to discard continues to be difficult for Emily as all things in her house embody memories; they are souvenirs or material remnants of another time and place, most importantly of her long life with Henry. On the occasion of the yearly rummage sale at her church, she goes through her things and wonders what to donate: "Hardest of all were those remnants of Henry's she should have thrown out years ago, like the matching luggage they'd bought for their trip to England—four hardshell American Tourister suitcases the dark purple of raw liver, each with its own gold monogram and combination lock. Tall and narrow, they hailed from the era before wheels, and had a tendency to topple over at the merest touch. . . . Since Henry died she hadn't used hers, as if breaking the set would be bad luck" (212–13). Emily remembers their trip to England—another predictable class-specific adventure that evidences her upper-middle-class and generation-specific profile—by way of their set of suitcases, which are themselves characteristic of a specific time and culture, that is, early American transatlantic mass tourism. As such, they are another symbol of mobility or, rather, past mobility. Emily realizes that she will never again travel farther than to her hometown outside Pittsburgh or, at best, Chautauqua Lake; not even to visit her granddaughters—in Chicago and Cambridge, Massachusetts, respectively—let alone to revisit Europe.

When Emily falls sick with a throat infection, it is Arlene who takes care of her, returning the favor, as it were: "She [Arlene] was enjoying playing nursemaid too much, and yet what a relief it was to cast off the last shreds of her dignity and surrender to her" (121). Whereas in *Wish You Were Here* Emily was still very critical of Arlene and jealous of her close relationship to Henry as well as to Margaret, over the years their everyday companionship has increasingly come to outweigh these points of contention; now, in old age, "they'd grown so yoked" (237).

Toward the end of the book spring returns (207) and with it the protagonist's longing for Henry: "what she missed most was the smell of his skin"

(207). She experiences a specific sense of loneliness and isolation due to the absence of particular bodily sensations. It is during a visit to Henry's grave—the chapter is titled "Hard to Kill"—that Emily's many conflicting emotions break forth. But even in this most intimate moment at the cemetery, Emily at first ponders questions of decorum and status. Surveying the plots of Pittsburgh's deceased notable residents—industrialists, architects, and artists—she is impressed and flattered at the same time: "Coming from Kersey, she'd thought it would be an honor to be buried here, and still did. As morbid as it sounded, she'd be proud, one day, to lie beside Henry" (238). Not even in the face of the dead (and anticipating her own death) can Emily entirely let go of her snobbery. The Maxwells' plot, "secured . . . with oil money" (239) by an ancestor of Henry's several generations ago, is ornamented with a flag signifying that Henry was a veteran. Emily is annoyed by this, mostly because it was put on the grave in her absence and without her knowledge. She acknowledges the graves of Henry's parents, Lillian and Gerald, and in her thoughts expresses her gratitude to Lillian: "She [Lillian] was so much what Emily had wanted to be, cultured and unflappable" (239). And she anticipates her own death and burial: "She would be on his right, replicating the way they slept" (240). Overexerting herself in the sun when watering the grave, Emily suffers a brief dizzy spell and is momentarily incapacitated: "Her vision dimmed, a shadow passing between her and the world" (242). Clinging to Henry's gravestone, she suddenly realizes that despite her earlier touch of melancholy, "she didn't want to die at all" (242) and begins to pull herself out of the daze, feels her pulse slow down, and returns to her senses. Recovered and composed once again, she stubbornly finishes what she came for: planting the grave. In one of the novel's wonderfully crafted key scenes, Emily lets down her guard and gives up all her usual impression management as she digs away at the grave: "She was sure that anyone watching would think she was a crazy woman. . . . She didn't care" (242). Liberated and determined, she continues her care work for the dead, planting cosmos flowers on her husband's grave. Emily's resilience prevails over her morbid thoughts and she comes out of the shadows with a renewed commitment to enjoy her life—or what remains of it—by spending time with her children and going on one more trip to Chautauqua Lake.

Even if the novel details the routine of Emily's life as an eighty-year-old widow, this life, as has become obvious, is not without its drama and its highs and lows. Emily is a modern heroine of the kind that Edith Wharton or Henry James could have invented in a younger and perhaps more tragic version in another time and place. In fact, "the spectre of Henry James hovers delicately above Emily's Grafton Street home, insinuating itself into O'Nan's spiraling, exact sentences and the beautiful, subtle symbolism that permeates the novel."[22] Emily has successfully moved up the social ladder; she is neither a rebel nor a feminist, and she has hardly ever questioned the status quo of the world around her—probably because she never had to. She occasionally may appear insensitive, even downright hard-hearted and complacent, yet her lack of too much self-doubt and her clear sense of knowing exactly how things are done in her little Pittsburgh universe may have also contributed to her longevity.

The novel ends as it began: with Emily and Arlene in the car sharing a ride, only this time it is Emily's car and she is sitting behind the wheel. They are on their way to Chautauqua for yet another family holiday week: "'And we're off!' Arlene said. 'Yes,' Emily said. 'We most certainly are'" (255). This is not a happy ending in the strict sense. The novel has, in fact, spelled out the impossibility of such a thing. Yet Emily and Arlene, as they are happily headed for the lake, are getting another chance at life.

THE THIRD NOVEL in the Maxwell series and the last one to be discussed in this chapter centers on Henry, who had been missing from the first two novels, as they are set after his death. In *Henry, Himself* (2019) he appears as an American everyman and as the patriarch of the Maxwell family. Not surprisingly, following O'Nan's dedication of *Emily, Alone* to his mother, *Henry, Himself* is dedicated to O'Nan's "father and his father before him." The novel is again set in Pittsburgh and at Chautauqua Lake and is as seemingly uneventful as its predecessors. Even if Henry's shadow loomed large in *Wish You Were Here* and *Emily, Alone,* it is in this prequel that the reader "meets" him for the first time. The pleasures of reading *Henry, Himself* partly stem from the fact that it is a fine novel in and of itself and partly from the joy of re-encountering the characters from the previous two Maxwell novels. Just as the two novels preceding its publication, "this is a novel that charms not through the complexities of its plot but through its subtle revelations of character and the human condition."[23] The novel is set in 1998—it begins on the last days of 1997 and ends on January 1, 1999—thus covering one year in Henry Maxwell's life with Emily. As in *Emily, Alone,* the overarching structure of the narrative is the calendar year, with its recurring events and occasions for family reunions. The novel is composed of eighty-four vignettes ranging in length from less than half a page to about fifteen pages; the average length is six to seven pages. At the time the novel is set, Henry is seventy-four years old; Emily is sixty-nine.

Literary critics have drawn various comparisons and analogies between *Henry, Himself* and a variety of more or less canonical works of American fiction: "The author evokes Henry's middle-class Pittsburgh existence like a Keystone State Joyce. One would have to go back to Evan S. Connell's *Mrs. Bridge* and *Mr. Bridge* to find a literary marriage bookended in such a perceptive fashion."[24] Connell's two novels (similarly written in an episodic style and adapted to film as *Mr. & Mrs. Bridge* in 1990) feature a likewise upper-middle-class family (in this case, in Kansas City) and through their protagonists—Mrs. Bridge in the 1959 novel and Mr. Bridge in the 1969 novel—capture a class- and period-specific American mentality. Deborah Donovan compares *Henry, Himself* to "Anne Tyler's character-driven novels set in Baltimore," and several reviewers liken O'Nan's protagonist to iconic literary figures in the works of John Updike and Richard Ford: "Though he's no Rabbit Angstrom or Frank Bascombe, Henry's inner life provides plenty of fertile territory for O'Nan to explore. For one thing, Henry's outward stoicism and his emotional instincts often appear to be at odds."[25] Another critic considers *Henry, Himself* "a John Updike *Rabbit* novel stripped to its bare essence."[26] *Henry, Himself,* seen as a novel of manners, chronicles Henry's life at church, at the country club, at the golf club, and in what is left of his social world in the city of Pittsburgh, of which he is a native. Henry is retired and no longer meets many of his old friends. Most of the time Emily is by his side. Like Emily, to whom he is by his own standards happily married, Henry is practiced in self-control and self-discipline, values that "his Brahmin upbringing" already (337) taught him (in contrast to Emily, who does not share his social upbringing). Henry remembers fondly how ignorant Emily was about table manners and class conventions when he first went out with her and introduced her to his parents: "His mother had liked her for trying, a small-town girl so obviously out of her depth, spreading butter on her roll at the club with her fish knife. As the lady of the house, his mother's gift was making everyone feel welcome" (65). Through Henry's eyes, the reader sees another side of Emily, yet Henry would never openly comment on her youthful lack of sophistication, which, as has become obvious in *Emily, Alone,* she has been trying all her life to overcome by overperforming the proper manners, taste, and demeanor. Still, the novel unveils a surprisingly rich inner life of a man who, to all outward appearances, is quietly observant and keeps to himself. At the same time, there is no heavy-handed symbolism in the novel, a text that, similar to its protagonist, operates in the register of subtle understatement: "O'Nan trusts that the simplicity of his story, rather than dulling Henry's character, will instead reveal it. Set against plain domestic backdrops, objects become practically radioactive with symbolic depth. A dusty old centerpiece evokes his mother. A useless roof aerial suggests a lost connection to his children. An ever-collapsing silverware drawer reminds him he'll always have problems—and a job to do."[27] Here, again, material things trigger the protagonist's memory and make him ponder the state of his relations with his family. Henry and Emily have always divided tasks and duties according to the separate-sphere model of gender roles they grew up with and have not deviated from it ever since Henry "proudly assumed his husbandly duty as dishwasher" (33) right after their honeymoon at Niagara Falls, an arrangement that—with intermissions—has continued into Henry's retirement. They get along well, for the most part, and occasionally also experience a deeper, romantic sense of devotion to each other, for instance, on the occasion of their anniversary or on Valentine's Day. "Marriage was about balance, about complementing each other" (26), Henry muses (rather than about self-realization, the reader may conclude). There is an undemanding air about Henry, who lives to please and accommodate every whim of Emily's—of which there are many. He is still baffled by her mood swings and by how opinionated and heartless she can appear. And still, "there's enduring love in this story. There's the lifelong romance between Henry and Emily, marked by prickly interludes and moments of sublime companionship. Their affectionate but flawed family is still part of their lives. O'Nan wisely refrains from dropping any narrative bombs into the story, leaving the characters to expand and fill the spaces. A wise, tender and humorous writer, he portrays outwardly unexceptional people with rich inner lives defined by doubt and anxiety, affection and hope."[28]

Not "dropping any narrative bombs" in an implicit way describes the slice-of-life aesthetic that informs *Henry, Himself* in the same way that it does many other novels by O'Nan. Over the course of the year narrated in the novel, which is structured by doctor's visits, family holidays, errands to the store, and tinkering in the garage, Henry seems rather at peace with himself. However, he too does observe and experience the consequences of old age: his increasing forgetfulness, his insecure driving (on the first pages of the novel, he almost causes an accident with a school bus), his physical pain (a knee injury, back pain, arthritis, and numb fingertips in the morning), and his intensifying intolerance for drink and food (he is overweight and still consumes alcohol on a daily basis). One chapter details his daily intake of pharmaceutical products since, "like most Americans their age, they took a lot of pills" (237). Three pages are spent chronicling the content of the medicine cabinet and the kinds of pills Henry is taking and in what kind of sequence before and after meals, concluding that "he was grateful, at his age, that there was nothing seriously wrong with him. Most of the time he felt fine" (239). The reader knows, however, that the many good intentions and New Year's resolutions Henry comes up with at the end of the novel will be for nothing as he is just about to become fatally ill. Knowing about Henry's impending end and considering all the things he does and says in that light—at least when we are familiar with the two preceding novels—may constitute the saddest instance of the everyday gothic, the dreadful lingering beneath the daily routine, we as readers are confronted with: "Knowing what happens in the future is almost a distraction from the story being told here but that knowledge most certainly enhances the poignancy of its conclusion."[29] In earlier scenes, it is already made clear that Emily, while having her own health issues, can be expected to outlive Henry; yet she is not at all amused when Henry makes half-joking comments in that direction. Emily's lack of humor at times bothers Henry, who tries to cope with death by belittling it—"Wasn't it better to laugh at death?" (11)—but in most situations he ignores it and simply goes back to his domestic tasks.

The marriage of the Maxwells does follow the norms of patriarchy, but with a twist. As has become obvious, Emily is hardly in an inferior position to Henry; many feminist scholars (such as Simone de Beauvoir) have pointed out that old age may generally flatten gender hierarchies and at times even invert them. Between Emily, who has always been a stay-at-home mom, and Henry, it is Henry who is more dependent on Emily for advice, for navigating social situations, and for organizing family meetings. Tellingly, "Sunday in the Maxwell household was call your mother day" (44), a ritual he has no part in: commonly, both Kenneth and Margaret call to speak to Emily, who then passes on information to Henry as she sees fit. As befits the separate-spheres logic they subscribe to, Henry does not share Emily's intense interest nor her emotional investment in the lives of their children and considers them grown and gone (and disappointments to varying degrees). When someone calls for Henry, it is mostly his sister Arlene needing him to fix something in her apartment, which he gladly does, as he is more than happy to demonstrate his usefulness (and to get out of the house occasionally).

Henry's dependence on Emily becomes quite obvious in several instances, such as when Emily moves in with her friend Louise for a couple of days to take care of her after she has had knee surgery and needs assistance. While the two friends enjoy spending time together, Henry, home alone, is jealous of their sisterhood but tries to persuade himself that "he was patient. He could wait. They'd been married almost fifty years. There was no point moping about like a lovesick teenager" (168). Eventually, in spite of his intentions to behave like an adult, he cannot resist going to Louise's house, where he tries to catch a glimpse of Emily through the window. In another instance, Emily goes to visit their daughter, Margaret, who has been in a car accident. With Kenneth, Lise, Sam, and Ella at the same time visiting their parents' home for Thanksgiving and the housewife gone, Henry feels uncomfortable in the role of host and overwhelmed by having to take over the kitchen. With Arlene's and Lise's help, the Thanksgiving dinner turns out well despite Emily's absence, which Henry is afraid might offend her: "While he'd missed her, it had been a good day. They'd all gotten along, but he couldn't say that" (336). Hence, his habitual reliance on Emily in all matters has created a situation in which even the smallest steps toward autonomy on his part might cause a domestic rift—thus emphasizing the threat any deviation from the ordinary poses for the established equilibrium.

Regarding their quotidian rituals, "O'Nan elevates the routines and chores of quiet domesticity to a nearly heroic level in his lingering attention to details, from plumbing troubles to coupons, walking the dog, and all the preparations and disruptions of holiday gatherings. Like Richard Russo and Anne Tyler, O'Nan discerningly celebrates the glory of the ordinary in this pitch-perfect tale of the hidden everyday valor of a humble and good man."[30] The drama in Henry's life is caused by the smallest of things. He, for example, observes a bird in the church during the Easter mass in Pittsburgh and bonds with his grandson over this unexpected apparition. In another instance he accidentally sees his daughter-in-law naked in the bathroom at their lake cottage. Visibly taken aback by the sight of Lise's naked breasts, his prudish reaction becomes a source of great entertainment for the family—yet "he didn't mind being the butt of the joke. A husband, he had practice" (209). Every time readers might think that the things occupying Henry's mind could not become more miniscule or banal, there is another instance to prove them wrong. This, at times, produces comic relief, for instance, when Henry during a holiday weekend at the cottage discovers that a family member forgot to flush the toilet—the section is titled "A Present" (219); Henry goes to great lengths to establish everyone's whereabouts and tries to guess who his predecessor in the bathroom could have been: "There were too few clues to reach a solution, yet his mind kept trying to make sense of it. As an engineer he was part detective, used to working backward from disaster" (220–21). For all of Henry's worrisome compliance and constant alertness, there are also small acts of resistance on his part. When Emily donates his mother's decorative grapes for the church rummage sale, he dutifully takes them to the bazaar but eventually buys them himself and takes them back home, where he hides them in the basement "where Emily would never find them" (160). The novel's representation of Henry's life in old age turns the very idea of a suspenseful plot and a gripping narrative on its head. As these examples show, Henry's attention to detail and propensity for obsessing over minutiae is quite impressive, showing perhaps the mind's capacity to create drama even where there is none and thus to preemptively fill the threatening void. But this disposition of his, on the other hand, also helps Henry take his mind off actually dramatic and serious events, for example, the death of his long-time physician, Dr. Runco, which comes as a shock to him.

The protagonist also is prone to revisit memories of his childhood and his life as a young man, even if this means reliving the frustrations and anxieties of the past. His mother named him after her brother who died in World War I and on Decoration Day used to take him, "Little Henry"—a nickname he did not appreciate—to the cemetery to visit his uncle's grave. Like his uncle, he would eventually go to war and fight in Europe, in World War II. Through the way that his war memories are presented in the novel, it becomes clear to the reader that he has been repressing them all his life and has never shared them with anybody, not even with Emily. Another painful memory of Henry's that he always kept to himself is that of Sloan, an upper-class woman with whom he had an affair shortly before he met Emily. When Sloan married and moved away, he was heartbroken. And long before both Emily and Sloan, there had been a long line of piano teachers Henry, as a boy, had been infatuated with. He is portrayed as quick to develop a crush and, once firmly committed, to be and to remain affectionately attached, no matter what. Even as their terms of engagement have changed—as a young man, he was first drawn to Emily because she flattered and admired him; now, in old age, her admiration has turned into worry and care—his attachment to Emily is unflagging and shown to have been reliable, constant, and pragmatic throughout their years together: "Who knew what happened in a marriage, what bargains and compromises people struck? He and Emily were opposites in many respects, yet well matched, both of them practical at heart" (186).

Not one to change his ways and habits easily or quickly, Henry is portrayed as a solid character who regularly appreciates his little comforts, among them those of food and drink. His taste characterizes him indirectly as having been shaped by the culture of a specific generation and class. Many of the dishes and cocktails that he and Emily are partial to evoke the upscale American consumer culture of the 1950s, partially reaching back to the late nineteenth century and including culinary signature dishes such as "lobster Benedict" and "bananas Foster" (93) or "chicken à la king" (40, 266). Rather than the contemporary common brand names the reader encounters in those novels by O'Nan that feature younger, mostly adolescent protagonists of a middle- or lower-middle-class background, food consumption is far more stylish with Henry and Emily, and it is hard to imagine that they would ever set foot in a Dunkin' Donuts or a McDonald's. These references in *Henry, Himself* to the specifics of cuisine help further establish Henry and Emily in their cultural particularity and class habitus, as is typical in a novel of manners.

And yet there is one aspect regarding Henry and the Maxwells in general that perhaps merits further inquiry as it often goes unnoticed and yet is highly relevant in the American context since it refers to the hidden normative center of American society: the Maxwells are white, and their whiteness is most meaningful in the context of the city of Pittsburgh and its thoroughly racialized neighborhoods. Whereas in his short story cycle *Everyday People* (2001) O'Nan has portrayed Pittsburgh's majority-black East Liberty neighborhood, his novels about the Maxwells also—albeit from a different angle and in often rather implicit ways—reveal the utterly segregated urban landscape of Pittsburgh and the country at large, if primarily by the usual absence of nonwhite people in the Maxwells' lives. Henry, for instance, notes with relief that he is "not the only white person" at the supermarket in a neighborhood that Emily should never even set foot in, according to his musings (35): "The East Liberty store was cramped and dirty, unimproved, like the neighborhood, a holdover from the fifties. His mother had shopped there for years, switching to Edgewood only after Martin Luther King was shot. Not that it was unsafe, but he wouldn't want Emily to go there alone this time of day" (34). Henry is here using language that is implicitly racial(ized), and the implicit racial bias he in this way betrays confirms his ignorance and his "racial meta-ignorance" (a term coined by José Medina[31])—that is, a form of active ignorance about all issues of race and (structural) discrimination. As racial meta-ignorance is part and parcel of white privilege, it is common with those who are not adversely impacted by racially defined social regulations. Henry, thus, can simply choose not to know anything about it: "Unlike aging characters by John Updike or Philip Roth, Henry doesn't explicitly grapple with or even reflect topical conflagrations. Perhaps Henry, himself, is temperamentally apolitical; but for Mr. O'Nan to note, as he does at one point, that Henry would "deny that he was a racist," and drop things there, seems to err too much on the side of kindness. This novel is a lovely tribute to the enduring mystery of an ordinary life; it wouldn't have hurt Henry much to hold him to stricter accounts on the matter."[32]

Their sense of entitlement and the kind of white privilege Henry and Emily take for granted reveal them to be beneficiaries of an order that puts other—that is, nonwhite—Americans at a disadvantage. From an African American studies perspective, one has to state, once again, that (just as in many fictional texts) it is the absence of the topic that is symptomatic for the ubiquity of racialization in U.S. society. In discussing the protagonist's unchallenged whiteness, we might need to inquire further into the role of nostalgia in *Henry, Himself* (and the Maxwell novels in general): "The gift of O'Nan's fiction is to immerse us deeply in Henry's essence, in his desire to be useful and his nostalgia for a vanished way of life, for the forgotten homespun rituals and for houses with slate roofs and ornate gables. And when we watch him winding the clocks forward, we find ourselves wishing he could hold the minute hand motionless for just a while longer."[33] Yet the nostalgia for a "vanished way of life" that permeates O'Nan's loving depictions of Pittsburgh and Chautauqua may not be so innocent after all and might contain the seeds of toxicity that is captured in Zygmunt Bauman's concept of "retrotopia."[34] After all, longing for the past and its seemingly stable social order implies a reluctance to deal with historical and contemporary questions of social justice. In that vein, Henry is reading a nonfiction book on the Lewis and Clark expedition, a historical event that, unlike any other, has been used to affirm a white settler-colonialist view of American history (133) without any concerns. It is only the later generations—Kenneth and Margaret and their children—that seem to question the status quo of their parents in new ways. Even if O'Nan deserves praise for "capturing America's shaky middle class with dignity and without flag-waving hagiography or overworked meaning-making," it is up to the reader to connect the fictional world his characters live in (and the world they long for) to the outside world, with its urging problems, and to interrogate their "habits of the heart" along with the uneasy connection between whiteness and nostalgia in these novels.[35]

CHAPTER 7

The Hollywood Novel Revisited

West of Sunset

Repeatedly, O'Nan has addressed historical settings and events in his writing. In *West of Sunset* (2015) he, for the first time, uses a historical figure as the main character in one of his novels. The fact that the person he chose is indeed an American icon, a "mythic persona"—namely, the writer F. Scott Fitzgerald—garnered the novel a lot of attention since popular and scholarly interest in the author and his works remains unabated.[1] Not only have Fitzgerald's novels been adapted to the big screen and the small screen numerous times, but his own life has been of continued interest for biographers and novelists. Several recent adaptations of Fitzgerald's works (such as the film *The Great Gatsby* in 2013 and the television series *The Last Tycoon* in 2016) and a continued interest in biographical matters—evidenced, for instance, in David S. Brown's 2017 biography *Paradise Lost: A Life of F. Scott Fitzgerald;* in the television series *Z: The Beginning of Everything* (2015), centering on Zelda Sayre as she meets, falls in love with, and marries F. Scott Fitzgerald; or in the German-language novel *Der Sommer, in dem F. Scott Fitzgerald beinahe einen Kellner zersägte* (2016) by British-Austrian writer Emily Walton, which centers on a vacation in France in March 1926 shortly after *The Great Gatsby* had been published—attest to the afterlives of Fitzgerald's fictional characters as well as to the manifold (re)interpretations of his life, his glamorous and tragic marriage with Zelda, and his legacy as a writer.

O'Nan's *West of Sunset* also returns to the life of the writer and offers a Hollywood novel with a twist, as it were—it is, at the same time, also a historical tale. The book centers, more specifically and perhaps somewhat anticlimactically in terms of glamour biography, on Fitzgerald's last years and "his third and final Hollywood venture," from 1937 to 1940—the year he died at age forty-four.[2] Struggling with alcoholism, financial hardship, and the separation from both his wife Zelda, who is in a mental institution in North Carolina, and his daughter, Scottie, who is attending a boarding school and later a college in the east, the once-famous writer has almost lost his spirits and no longer enjoys celebrity status (he has literally "fallen from his jazz-age fame"[3]). Yet his faith in his own abilities as a writer is unfaltering, and he appears to be starting over when he moves back to Hollywood to write and redact screenplays while also working on his next novel, *The Love of the Last Tycoon,* which will remain unfinished and will be published posthumously by Edward Wilson in 1941 as *The Last Tycoon*. The first epigraph for *West of Sunset* is drawn from this text: "There are no second acts in American lives"—a sharp counterpoint to the second epigraph of the novel, "nothing was impossible—everything was just beginning," which is taken from Fitzgerald's short story "Crazy Sunday."[4] Taken together, the epigraphs comment on the notion of a second chance, part and parcel of the American Dream and prominently addressed in Fitzgerald's iconic *The Great Gatsby*. Whether Fitzgerald will be able to start over is the question that hovers over the entire novel, at times evoking optimism and hope, at times doom and failure.

West of Sunset—the title referencing the Los Angeles' neighborhood that houses the film studios: West of Sunset Boulevard—joins the ranks of Hollywood novels such as Nathanael West's *The Day of the Locust* (1939; a novel that is even mentioned in O'Nan's book, as it is just published at the time and was brought to Fitzgerald's attention), Norman Mailer's *Deer Park* (1955), or Joan Didion's *Play It as It Lays* (1970), to name but a few. The Hollywood novel has been notoriously hard to define as it spans various literary and popular texts that choose the film industry in Hollywood as both subject and setting. Nancy Brooker-Bowers, who has compiled the most comprehensive bibliography of the subgenre, sees it as "an American regional fictional genre that features characters that work in the film industry either in Hollywood or with a Hollywood production company on location."[5] John Parris Springer describes the Hollywood novel as exploring Hollywood's "symbolic role" in national culture and dubs it "the best and the worst in American life."[6] Springer offers a useful typology of specific characters, settings, and scenes that are in part also realized in O'Nan's book: among the characters are "the avaricious producer, the libidinal starlet, the ambitious director, the disillusioned writer, the down-and-out extra."[7] Fitzgerald in O'Nan's rendering clearly belongs into the category of the disillusioned writer. But rather than to indulge the stereotypes of the Hollywood novel, O'Nan operates at a critical distance to them, an aloofness that is already built into his fictional portrait of the historical author. As Fitzgerald's biographers have noted, the writer is dismayed by the factory atmosphere and the collaborative work style. O'Nan draws out Fitzgerald's reluctance to cowrite with others and his outright rejection of any changes to the scenes he has crafted so meticulously, changes which he has to endure nonetheless, being merely a "Hollywood Hack" who has no authority whatsoever over his own text.[8] Hired to write, he delivers what is asked of him—or not quite: often, he misses deadlines, and he is still finishing scripts for films that have already been shelved by the producers, which makes him painfully aware of the futility of his creative work. All the while, he works on the *Tycoon* in his spare time. Next to the typical characters of the Hollywood novel, Springer also identifies typical scenes and settings, that, again, also structure O'Nan's novel, such as "the Hollywood party, the story conference or production meeting, the studio back lot, the Hollywood premiere."[9] The Hollywood novel predominantly portrays the film industry in an ambivalent light and offers a behind-the-scenes look at the dream factory, exposing the often negative effects it has on the lives of those who are part of it. It critiques the short-dated hypes and the superficiality of the film business—how it uses (up) talents and swiftly disposes of them, how it turns people into stars and stars into expendable entities. In his own life, Fitzgerald experienced the upward and downward spiraling of the Hollywood circuit several times in quick succession. O'Nan's portrayal seems to suggest that Hollywood is a highly ambivalent place for Fitzgerald to the bitter end: it enables him to tap into his old network, to make a living, and to find some sort of temporary home while also offering the ideal environment for "normalizing" his self-destructive life style that includes drug abuse and a habitual alcoholism of the kind he had fallen prey to long ago.

Apart from reimagining Fitzgerald's last years, *West of Sunset* also takes great pains to (re)construct a rich tapestry of the milieu and the time in an interplay of historicity and fictionality typical of historical fiction: the novel features contemporaneous stars such as Dorothy (Dotty) Parker, Humphrey Bogart, Joan Crawford, Marlene Dietrich, and, of course, Ernest Hemingway and has them engage in sharp-tongued dialogues and much interpersonal innuendo. Even off screen, they appear to be playacting around each other, and their interactions seem to be driven by narcissism, envy, resentment, and cynicism. O'Nan's kaleidoscope of Hollywood in the 1930s plays against the onset of war in Europe (Thomas Mann and Lion Feuchtwanger, the two German writers in L.A. exile, make a brief appearance at a party), on the one hand, and against the backdrop of "the Crash" of 1929, whose repercussions are still felt all around, on the other hand. It almost seems as if recurring references to 1929 and the national economic collapse foreshadow the eventual collapse of the protagonist.

Central to the constellation of characters in terms of rivalry is the Fitzgerald–Hemingway axis. Time and again, it is Hemingway against whom Fitzgerald measures his own achievements and failures. The re-encounter with Hemingway early in the novel superficially characterizes their relationship as casual and distant at the same time. In February, March, and April 1936, Fitzgerald had published the "Crack-Up"-triptych in *Esquire,* three articles in the confessional mode about his life as a writer in "a raw and painful public portrait" that shows him as a member of the "lost (or "half-lost") generation" but also earned him much criticism from his colleagues (the novel refers to the articles as "those mea culpas"; 3).[10] Hemingway, above all, caricatures Fitzgerald in a side remark in his short story "The Snows of Kilimanjaro," a piece published also in *Esquire* in August 1936, calling him "wretched," and it is against the backdrop of this "exchange" that *West of Sunset* stages their meeting. On the surface, it seems to be Hemingway who is deranged and injured while he concedes to Fitzgerald: "You look well" (32); yet between the lines it becomes obvious that Hemingway is now the successful star (who can afford to disappear without a word from a party given in his honor and who can treat his colleague in a condescending fashion) while Fitzgerald exists and works at the mercy of his Hollywood mentors.

O'Nan's Hollywood novel portrays Fitzgerald writing a Hollywood novel, and it is this metafictional dimension that produces a doubling and mirroring effect. In the end, however, the novel leaves the myths of both Golden Age Hollywood and of F. Scott Fitzgerald as troubled genius intact, with both mutually re-enforcing each other. Critics have appreciated the novel as an homage to Fitzgerald as well as to Los Angeles: "This book is catnip for aficionados of prewar L.A. and Fitzgerald fetishists";[11] *West of Sunset* has even garnered praise as "the best Golden Age Hollywood novel to come down Sunset Boulevard in years."[12]

But O'Nan did not intend to cash in on an imitation of Fitzgerald's style; contrary to the claims of some reviewers, he explicitly states: "I knew that I couldn't do his actual voice, or try to use his exact words. I didn't want to imitate his style. You can't write Fitzgerald as well as Fitzgerald wrote Fitzgerald for any length of time. So I knew I wanted to do it in third person, and use the authorial voice to tell the story. I tried to get at his sensibility by reading both his fiction and his nonfiction, and by reading his letters."[13] It is only in short passages of fictional letters (set in italics) that O'Nan actually tries to recreate the voices of his main characters: Fitzgerald, Zelda, and their daughter, Scottie. These made-up letters, for one, are to convey Fitzgerald's relentless endeavor to put up a brave front for Zelda and Scottie, to assure both of his devotion, and to share illusionary plans for their future, in which Zelda would have recovered and they would be reunited as a family, a future in which Fitzgerald has less and less faith and investment.

Spread out evenly in nineteen chapters, the book not only introduces historical personae of the Hollywood scene, examines Fitzgerald's relationship to them, and digs deep into the Fitzgerald-archive, it also, almost en passant, references many details from everyday life in the 1930s, including cultural events and developments in the city. Fitzgerald and his newfound Hollywood love, Sheilah Graham, watch Kenny Washington, the first African American player in the National Football League, play for the L.A. Bruins; they also take a boat to Santa Catalina Island to spend the day as tourists, contemplate breakfast at Tom Breneman's, and visit the World's Fair in San Francisco in 1939. *West of Sunset* comes with a representation of the cultural history of the 1930s and evokes images of art deco architecture (such as the Thalberg Building, in which Fitzgerald goes to work) and leisurely car rides across the city, up into the Hollywood hills, to Santa Monica, or to Encino. This situatedness of the plot (Los Angeles of the 1930s, in O'Nan's prose, becomes as realistically vivid as contemporary Pittsburgh does in the trilogy of the Maxwell family) generates an authenticity effect and a verisimilitude that adds to the book being more than a formulaic Hollywood novel or another fictional hagiography of Fitzgerald, the writer.

Throughout, the physical, economic, and social vulnerability of the writer and the precariousness of his family are dwelt upon. The novel opens up by introducing the fragility of the lives of Scott and Zelda, after the fall, so to speak: Scott's drinking and Zelda's mental condition, for which she is in institutional care, have taken their toll. Bypassing their whirlwind romance and their iconic couplehood of "another age" (5), the reader's first glimpse of the couple is on their seventeenth anniversary when Zelda's doctor allows Fitzgerald to take her on an outing to Chimney Rock, outside Asheville, North Carolina. This excursion elucidates and emphasizes their deep bond but also introduces the fact that Fitzgerald finds her more of a stranger every time he visits, with only momentary recognition of their past intimacy; together they seem "the king [and queen] of things going wrong" (9).

While caring long distance for Zelda, O'Nan's Fitzgerald falls in love again after his arrival in Los Angeles, with Sheilah Graham, "a gossip columnist" (42) who will eventually take care of him when his health deteriorates. Still, his mind is on Zelda, whom he continues to visit and provide for, but the couple's last hope that eventually "she would be sane. He would be sober" (244) is never realized. Ultimately, the fictionalized Fitzgerald is able to concede that "they had been so miserable together that he'd never invented a happy ending for them" (251). Contrary to revisionist feminist scholarship on the famous couple,

O'Nan does not portray Zelda as a victim who, first exploited and later abandoned by her husband, was pathologized and institutionalized for her resistance to then-dominant gender regimes.[14] Rather, the novel portrays Zelda and F. Scott's relationship as a sad and tragic love story and shows Fitzgerald as overwhelmed by and helpless in the face of his wife's mental condition, harboring strong feelings of remorse and regret. Certainly, "O'Nan is most convincing when he conveys the heartbreaking guilt Fitzgerald feels about having left Zelda behind in so many ways."[15] In O'Nan's novel it is Zelda rather than her husband who is granted the last word (in a letter to her daughter relating "some difficulties owing to real rather than imagined sadness" [289]). Of course, one may debate whether O'Nan's text produces poetic justice in his treatment of the couple and their marriage or delivers realistic literary portraits of them. Toward the end of the novel and the end of his life, the fictional Fitzgerald sees his increasing dependency on Sheilah mirroring his relationship to Zelda: He is as rigorously controlled and disciplined by his lover as Zelda is in her institution, and he considers this to be somewhat ironic. At first, as he falls in love with Sheilah, he manages to keep the drinking at bay, spending as much time with her as possible, and notes "on average he hadn't been this sober in years" (158). He becomes not only her lover but also her teacher of literature and poetry, and jokingly they call it their "college of one." Graham later published her own memoirs of their relation under exactly this title.[16] Still, his relapses are dramatic, and in his alcoholic stupor he repeatedly turns against those he loves. Sheilah, who has her own white lies and eventually reveals to him her "Dickensian past" (124), recoils from his drunken improprieties and withdraws. A weekend in Hanover, New Hampshire, on the campus of Dartmouth College, costs him one of his last engagements, one that he had relied upon to help him cover his financial obligations and secure future employment. Jason Tanz refers to this episode as a "lost weekend" in a *New York Times* article, echoing the title of Billy Wilder's film of an unsuccessful writer drinking himself into a stupor.[17]

As Fitzgerald's health rapidly deteriorates, he is struggling to finish his novel, lying in bed, propped up just enough to write on a board. *West of Sunset* dramatizes these last days and weeks as a race against time since several heart palpitations bordering on heart attacks emphasize his utter frailty. On his deathbed, O'Nan has him succinctly protest the ill timing of his own death: "*But I'm not done*" (288), thus granting Fitzgerald one final illusion or one last glimpse at the green light, if we are to use the central metaphor in his masterpiece *The Great Gatsby*.

CHAPTER 8

Other Works

Due to the limited scope of this study, not every work by Stewart O'Nan could be discussed at length; those texts that have not been treated in the previous chapters are acknowledged at least briefly in this chapter.

Stewart O'Nan's career began with the publication of the short story collection *In the Walled City* in 1993. The stories in this collection already indicate the diverse interests and the broad scope of the author. The prize-winning book features twelve stories that center on a variety of characters as diverse as an old Chinese grocer, a farmer facing financial ruin, a black day laborer, and a young policeman—"all of them vividly alive and different from the rest, yet mysteriously joined by the author's feel for the weight of the histories they carry."[1] Many of the stories in this volume are plot stories that often end in or with an act of violence: a farmer—out of desperation—commits murder-suicide, killing himself and his family ("Calling"); a policeman, unable to get over his divorce, shoots his ex-wife ("Winter Haven"). In many instances, the desperation of O'Nan's characters in combination with their easy access to firearms generates tragedy and resonates profoundly with the present moment in American society. However, these stories are balanced to some degree by more optimistic ones dealing with individuals who attempt to—and manage to—change their lives, to start over, and to begin again: for example, by getting a new job, learning to drive, or reconciling with loved ones.

Neither a short story collection nor a novel but more specifically a short story cycle, *Everyday People* (2001) is set in East Liberty, a majority-black neighborhood in Pittsburgh: "O'Nan invents and enters the poor African-American Pittsburgh neighborhood of East Liberty in the fall of 1998. Cutting back and forth among various points of view over the course of an ordinary week, O'Nan is a tender witness to the quotidian struggles of his creations."[2]

Through its urban setting of Pittsburgh, the book appears slightly analogous to other books that focus on specific neighborhoods and their social dynamics, such as Edward P. Jones's short story collection *Lost in the City* (1992), which is set in Washington, D.C., or Gloria Naylor's *The Women of Brewster Place* (1982), also dubbed a short story cycle,[3] which is set in a housing development in an unnamed city. Like Naylor's female protagonists, who are facing a wall in Brewster Place, O'Nan's neighborhood is similarly walled off after an expressway has been built to detour out-of-town traffic, literally cutting off East Liberty from the rest of the city, rendering its name highly ironic. "The Wall" here is a symbol of segregation and ghettoization, and yet it may also be a space of resistance and protest: "Sometimes The Wall glows in the dark. When it rains the colors shine brighter. People say you can see Martin Robinson crying, and at night they say Malcolm bleeds. Folks go down and touch it, leave things, notes and such, pictures of loved ones. It's not enough, but it's something. You're never going to get a square deal, not in this city."[4]

One of the characters, Chris Tolbert, who is paralyzed after an accident at "The Wall" that had killed his friend, is working on a mural to document and commemorate the history of this particular neighborhood and its people. Hence, "The Wall" is turned from an obstacle and a barrier into an archive. Vanessa, Chris's former girlfriend and mother of little Rashaan (Chris's son), is going back to college, and her first assignment is an oral history project in a class on African American history, which has her realize that black intellectual history offers her an interpretive framework for her present. She is turning the archive into a knowledge-to-live-by. Both Chris and Vanessa, with their aesthetic and intellectual work, embody the hopes of a community that is portrayed mostly as the place of violence, alienation, and loneliness.

Of course the literary representation of African American characters by a white author may be seen as very problematic from an African American perspective and may be read as necessarily producing misrepresentation, as Toni Morrison has amply shown in her *Playing in the Dark: Whiteness and the Literary Imagination* (1992), but reviewers voiced no accusations of O'Nan "culturally appropriating" an African American neighborhood. The following quote by Stacey D'Erasmo seems to point—quite to the contrary—to a kind of authorial restraint that might be fostered by political correctness: "Though this is a character-driven book, the everyday people of the title have a muted, small quality, like figures cut out of felt. While the one who shaped them is undeniably kind, he seems to have forgotten to give them any interesting edges. . . . O'Nan appears to have been waylaid in his fictional mission by the sneakiest of demons: politeness. Tentative, almost fatally respectful, he treats his characters very gingerly, as if he were afraid he might break them."[5] In *In the Walled*

City, O'Nan experimented with different voices and protagonists of different ethnicities and thus conjured different sociocultural milieus; *Everyday People* may in this regard even exceed his earlier book in that it "evokes a whole world by walking only a few blocks," featuring an ensemble of characters who keep reappearing in the course of interrelated events in their neighborhood.[6] To describe this book as a short story cycle rather than as a novel (as some critics have done) is to accentuate the loose connections among the characters and the episodic quality of each chapter. While their sequence matters greatly and while there is somewhat of a narrative frame encompassing all of the tales, each story holds its own.

In the screenplay *Poe* (2008), written for a bio-pic about Edgar Allan Poe, O'Nan revisits the nineteenth-century writer's tortured life and unpacks its tragedies, admitting that he, in fact, had never been an avid reader of Poe's literary works but developed a renewed interest in him through the twentieth-century horror genre, "the imaginary Poe of B movies."[7] Undoubtedly, Poe in the cultural imagination has become thoroughly intertwined with his work, as if his texts were all purely autobiographical or he himself were a character in his stories. It is this kind of transference that O'Nan's screenplay is teasing out. Being a gothic writer of sorts himself, O'Nan clearly shares some of Poe's approach to settings and character constellations. In this vein, *A Face in the Crowd* (2012, cowritten with Stephen King) is a gothic novella featuring a protagonist who, when watching baseball on television, begins to see familiar faces in the bleachers—faces of people he not only knew personally but also knows to be dead. This phenomenon through its presentation in the story appears as straddling the everyday gothic and traditional gothic horror. O'Nan and Stephen King had already collaborated previously on a baseball-related project with the self-explanatory title *Faithful: Two Diehard Boston Red Sox Fans Chronicle the Historic 2004 Season* (2004), which includes O'Nan's coverage of the games in the vivid style of radio sportscasters and announcers such as Bob Prince and Nellie King, who he listened to as a boy, whereas Stephen King provides commentaries to the games. Critics have pointed out that "the book is written in fluent baseball-ese, a language containing references to the DH rule and such mysterious descriptors as the 4–6-3 DP. The cast of characters is bigger than in many of King's miniseries, and major players vanish in mid-season to be replaced by newcomers."[8] The analogy between the championship and a television drama points to the shared ground between sports reportage and suspenseful fiction—if you know the codes. Reviewers concede that the entertainment value of the book in part hinges on readers' familiarity with baseball: "On the downside, the book is filled with the kind of facts and figures that baseball—and cricket—fans lap up and can reel off at will, but that baffle the rest of us. In places, too, the insider's jargon is so impenetrable it could almost be written in another language: 'Ortiz busts out of his slump with a tater over the Sox bullpen in the first . . . in the third, Manny retaliates with a three-run opposite field shot.' . . . One can, though, simply skip over this stuff and get to the real meat: the emotional rollercoaster ride that accompanies the Sox historic and, characteristically, tortuous path to victory."[9]

Apart from sports, war is another theme that permeates O'Nan's oeuvre. His texts represent war as a most impactful experience that has shaped the lives of men (and women) greatly throughout American history. Jacob Hansen in *A Prayer for the Dying* is a Civil War veteran who cannot find postwar peace (see chapter 2). *A World Away* (1998), a novel set in the 1940s that O'Nan has described as an American pastoral, depicts the lives of James and Anne Langer, for whom World War II is distant until their son, Rennie, who is fighting in the Pacific, returns home severely injured in both mind and body. Henry Maxwell, in *Henry, Himself,* deals with the family trauma of World War I (in which his uncle died) and his own traumatic experiences of World War II (see chapter 6). Larry Markham, in *The Names of the Dead* (1996), is a Vietnam veteran who is stalked by another former soldier, Ronald Creeley—victim of child abuse, trained assassin, and troubled veteran—who has escaped from a psychiatric ward. The novel interlaces Larry's post-Vietnam life in upstate New York in the early 1980s with a combat narrative set in Vietnam. "When is this Vietnam crap going to be over?," Larry's wife, Vicky, asks him before she leaves him for good, and it seems to be a rhetorical question.[10] Unsurprisingly, it is the war in Vietnam that O'Nan deals with most extensively in his writings, as he witnessed its repercussions himself as he was growing up. He often returns to what he calls "the gap" between veterans and civilians, that is, the much-deplored chasm between those who have experienced the "chaos of war" and those who "don't or won't understand."[11] In *The Vietnam Reader* (1998), O'Nan, as editor, has brought together a rich collection of more than seven hundred pages of Vietnam writing—from poems and song lyrics (including Bruce Springsteen's "Born in the USA" [1984]) to memoirs and postmodern prose (including excerpts from Tim O'Brien's *The Things They Carried* [1990]). The anthology addresses a larger public and was originally put together by O'Nan for the purpose of teaching the Vietnam War in college—hence the inclusion of a glossary, chronology of events, and reading questions. For the explicitly didactic purposes of reducing or even closing the above-stated gap and overcoming the unspeakability of the war experience, it provides "both an essential overview and a deep understanding how America has seen its time in Vietnam over the past thirty years."[12] The editor, however, concedes that its scope is "restricted to American views of the war," a fact that is not least reflected in the collected texts' recurring representations of the prototypical American hero-soldier: "The soldier and later the vet are often given to the reader as types, if not stereotypes already familiar to the casual reader or viewer. Here's a brief list: professional warrior, reluctant draftee, terrified new guy, hardened grunt, psycho killer/psycho vet, deluded lifer, bumbling ROTC lieutenant, disabled protest vet, troubled/addicted vet. Of course these end up being reductive if not outright slanderous clichés, but the reader will recognize variations on all these characters throughout this book and should be aware of them, and also of who on that list is eligible to play the American hero, and why."[13]

The anthology also samples a section from O'Nan's own *The Names of the Dead* (1996); the passage chosen for inclusion is set at the Vietnam Veterans Memorial in Washington, D.C. (to which the novel's title is an obvious reference). Reminiscent of the ending of Bobbie Ann Mason's novel *In Country* (1985), of which an excerpt is also featured in the anthology, O'Nan's protagonist drives to Washington, D.C., with his little son to visit the Vietnam Memorial on the National Mall. In both novels, the visit to the memorial creates a multigenerational experience of healing and closure: "This time Larry wouldn't miss anyone. This time he would bring them all home."[14]

A Good Day to Die (1999), published under the pseudonym James Coltrane, is a speculative thriller set in Cuba shortly after the death of Fidel Castro. More than any of his other novels, it adheres to the genre conventions of the thriller and of spy fiction and shares similarities with works by Graham Greene and Tom Clancy. The protagonist, Jorge Ortega, is a Cuban American secret operative whose grandfather died during the failed Bay of Pigs invasion. After missions in El Salvador, Belize, Nicaragua, Kuwait, and Vietnam, which he remembers as a series of lingering "bad dreams," Ortega is sent to the Cuban town of Santa Rosa with orders to join a group of rebels, take over a local radio station, and coordinate with a larger U.S. invasion force.[15] It is not quite clear whether Ortega and his men are being used as pawns to be sacrificed for reasons they do not know or understand. At the same time he is still haunted by memories of Catalina, a Salvadorian woman he fell in love with on a previous mission, who was tortured and killed.[16] In Santa Rosa he has an affair with Gloria, who is part of the guerrilla group he has joined. The group is torn by internal dissent, and upon Ortega's arrival, cultural misunderstandings add to an already volatile situation. Ortega attempts to assert himself as leader of the group and throughout the novel embodies, as reviewers have pointed out, the classical characteristics of genre-specific, hard-boiled masculinity: vulnerable and traumatized on the inside, he appears tough and cynical on the outside and acts accordingly. In an interview, O'Nan likened the novel to Ernest Hemingway's *For Whom the Bell Tolls* (1940), with which it shares some obvious similarities (despite the protagonists' opposed ideological positions)—Hemingway's protagonist, Robert Jordan, fights with a guerrilla group in the Spanish Civil War and falls in love with a woman in the group.[17] Moreover, Hemingway's novel covers seventy hours during an operation to destroy a bridge, and O'Nan's narrative is likewise time-compressed, recalling the Hemingway code of "grace under pressure."[18] With its setting, O'Nan's novel also thrives on little doses of revolutionary romanticism and Cuban exoticism.[19] By publishing the novel under a pseudonym, O'Nan himself seems to imply that this is the odd one out among his writings; it is in any case a text that, unlike all his others, does actually move very little beyond the well-worn paths of formula fiction.

The Circus Fire: A True Story of an American Tragedy (2000) is a nonfiction book that reconstructs the catastrophe of the July 6, 1944, Hartford circus fire, which left 167 people dead (mostly women and children) and many hundreds more injured. O'Nan estimates that approximately 8,700 people were in attendance of the Ringling Bros. and Barnum & Bailey Circus show that day.[20] Drawing on eyewitness accounts of survivors and including a wealth of additional material (photographs, police reports, court records), the book offers a comprehensive account of the tragedy. O'Nan was drawn to studying the event when, after moving to Hartford, Connecticut, in the 1990s, he realized how pivotal this singular event has been in shaping the cultural memory of the city and, in fact, Hartford's inhabitants continued to be haunted by it. In the absence of a full-fledged account or definitive history of it, O'Nan began to interview resident survivors of the tragic event, and he went into the archive, eventually becoming the chronicler of the circus fire. His book, after documenting several similar though less dramatic fires that preceded the one in Hartford, gives a detailed account of the gruesome events of July 6 (the site of the fire is likened to a war battlefield; as there were too few emergency exists, audience members got trampled by the panicked crowd) and the long aftermath. O'Nan traces the event's impact on both the personal lives of circus employees and local residents, its decades-long police investigation (the fire's cause could never be definitively established), and the lawsuits filed against the circus company (which eventually resulted in moderate settlement payments and a few short sentences for negligence). More specifically, O'Nan shows how earlier accounts of the event, by focusing on a few cases of individual heroism (possibly involving one case of mistaken identity), have partially overshadowed the memory of the many lives that ended that day and have also done little to shed light on the many unanswered questions surrounding the incident. While he does not brush over the well-documented stories of the heroes and heroines, he also seeks to expand the event's history and its commemoration by including stories of trauma and remembrance of following generations, and he calls into question the possibility of ever arriving at a conclusive account of what happened: "As for the mysteries of the circus fire—the missing and unidentified, the possibility of arson—they will probably always be mysteries, unsolved and unredeemed. Likewise, the desire to make sense of what happened, to find some justice and peace of mind by ordering and documenting the events, will always tempt us. But the fire is not that kind of story. Look close and it breaks up, it falls apart."[21] The tragedy of the circus fire with its lingering specter of uncertainty yet again evokes the everyday gothic in this nonfiction text. O'Nan renders in graphic and at times "excruciating detail" what we do know, "offering an engaging verisimilitude," yet he also discusses the event's many unknowns at length, creating a stark und unsettling contrast between both.[22]

In the vein of the much earlier *A Good Day to Die* (1999), O'Nan's 2016 *City of Secrets* is his second novel that is entirely set outside the United States and likewise explores espionage, terrorism, and romance. The book is a noir thriller that takes inspiration from quite a number of popular authors: "Chandler, Hammett, Le Carré, and Orson Welles come to mind."[23] The novel is set in post–World War II Jerusalem, and the protagonist, Jossi Brand, is a Jewish-Latvian camp survivor who has lost his entire family in the Nazi killing machinery and who is now part of an underground network spinning political intrigue and engaging in acts of terrorism against the British administrators/occupiers of Mandatory Palestine. The novel culminates in a fictionalized rendering of the King David Hotel bombing, which took place on July 22, 1946, and killed close to one hundred people. Brand as a character is morally ambiguous as he has to make "moral choices around the use of political violence" (see the appendix) that are further complicated by his love for Eva, a fellow conspirator and somewhat of a femme fatale. It is his fatalistic worldview as much as any real conviction that guides his actions: "He wasn't weak enough to kill himself, but wasn't strong enough to stop wanting to."[24] Brand is caught between careless resignation and the desire for meaning and a mission in his life. In an age of global terrorism, O'Nan's novel reminds us of terrorism's historical depth and various origins, but it is highly localized since it also "illuminates a past that reveals much about Jerusalem and the rest of the Middle East of today."[25]

PAST HIS TWENTY-FIVE-YEAR anniversary as a writer of fiction, Stewart O'Nan has remained astonishingly versatile and delightfully unpredictable. For all the diversity of his texts, this study has identified recurring themes and settings, techniques, and modes of literary representation as well as influences and genealogies that shape his oeuvre and partially hold it together. In terms of topics and subjects, his work continues to speak to the current moment in American (cultural) history.

This book may serve as an introduction to and a critical overview of Stewart O'Nan's works, and I am confident that it constitutes only the first step of many toward a more substantial critical assessment of his writings. This study is, above all, an invitation to read and to discuss O'Nan's work as the rich and vivid constituent of the literary archive of the American cultural imaginary, and, as that, it undoubtedly deserves to be appreciated.

APPENDIX

"I Don't Stop at the Sentimental"—An Interview with Stewart O'Nan

1. Which role did literature (or reading as such) play in your home/family when you were growing up? What kinds of books did you read and/or enjoy as a kid? (You mention Bradbury in an interview about The Night Country, *and I have come across a few other names, but perhaps you can say a little more about your own "formative" reading). What do you remember reading in school?*

My mother was a big reader—mostly polite British mysteries, like those of Dorothy L. Sayers and Ngaio Marsh. While the downstairs bookshelf was crammed with classics (Shakespeare, the Greek tragedies, the Brontës, Dostoevsky, Turgenev, Dickens), for her nightly reading she preferred lighter fare. My first love was comic strips in the daily newspaper, and Charles M. Schulz's *Peanuts* was my favorite. It still seems brilliant to me, his ability to get across the mixed emotions of everyday life in just four panels. I also loved horror comics, reading them at our local newsstand the day they were released. My first big binge read was Edgar Rice Burroughs's *Tarzan* series. I bought a whole box of them at a Cub Scout rummage sale for ten cents apiece and systematically devoured them. But I was also influenced by lots of sixties and seventies TV shows like *The Twilight Zone,* and horror movies like *Night of the Living Dead,* made right here in Pittsburgh by George A. Romero. The only thing I remember reading in school as a child is *The Phantom Tollbooth.* Much later, in middle school, we were reading *Julius Caesar,* memorizing Marc Antony's funeral speech, and I was so bored that I opened a book I found on the shelves in the back of the class, a book meant for older students: *A Clockwork Orange.*

2. *What do you see as the role of literature today, for instance in public life in America? Is there one? Should there be one?*

Literature has two roles, one public and one private. When we read anything, it's a private act, and we're entertained or informed or moved individually. But what a piece of literature stands for and how it's viewed by the masses and disseminated to them by the media is a very public thing. Certain books and authors are seen as important or significant culturally, just like certain movies, and then there are those that are just marketing successes—"big" books like *The DaVinci Code* or *The Goldfinch*—that take their place in our pop culture. The literature that changes our lives is personal, but sometimes it's delivered to us by much larger outside forces.

3. *War is a recurring theme in your work, all kinds of wars, in fact: The Civil War, World War II, Vietnam. In* Everyday People, *"war" also references the situation in the inner-city in the U.S. What kinds of wars do you see going on right now?*

Having grown up in the U.S. during the Vietnam War and the social revolutions of the sixties, I'm drawn to war and revolution in my work, looking at the battle lines even in my quieter, more domestic books. The wars I see right now are the ones built into the U.S. and also contemporary Western culture: the individual versus the collective and the questions of who is included, who is excluded, and whether there is a moral way to challenge or change that. The difficulty of empathy and understanding across race, class, gender, and religions.

4. *Repeatedly, your texts start off with diagnosing the lack of perspective perceived by teenagers in their hometowns. Simple boredom has them do stupid things. Experiences of initiation easily can lead to death or trauma. In that sense, how dangerous is it to grow up in America today?*

I think with social media it's harder now to be a private person, and that that makes the gauntlet of growing up that much harder. The models for who and what you can be now as a young person are wider than before, but it's a rare place (anywhere) that isn't narrow, and the current climate here, culturally, is mean, and tough on anyone who's different.

5. *Even if not all of your works follow a gothic mode, the uncanny seems to be always close at hand. There is a kind of "everyday gothic" in your writing that reveals itself in small things (such as the mysterious gas station robbery in* Wish You Were Here*). How do you create this atmosphere of the everyday gothic and to what purpose? Is there a sense of lingering discomfort you would like to convey to your readers?*

Maybe it's my roots in horror, but there seems to be all kinds of weird and deadly stuff around us. The quietest, safest neighborhood in Pittsburgh is Squirrel Hill, where I went to high school, and that's where that right-wing maniac killed eleven people at Tree of Life synagogue. People are arrested for child porn every day here, and priests and teachers are accused of molesting children. Mothers kill their children, husbands kill their wives. People are secretive and creepy and capable of awful things. As Denis Johnson says: "There's all this stuff inside us and it wants to come out."

6. I am struck with the ways in which you successfully skirt the sentimental in your work (which seems to be the default mode of representation in much of American literature), even when you address personal, intimate matters. Would you consider yourself an "unsentimental" or even "antisentimental" writer?

I think I'm as sentimental as most writers, but I don't stop at the sentimental, I go further and discover something on the other side that's disturbing (as in *A Prayer for the Dying,* in which Jacob's love for his family won't let him let go of them even after their deaths) or just vexing (as in *Emily, Alone,* in which her idealized love for her children is complicated by reality).

7. Prompted by some of the allusions and references in your work (in Prayer, *for instance), I want to ask you about intertextual references to the Bible. How important are they in your work and do they call for a well-versed reader? Can a knowledge of biblical stories (still) be taken for granted with a contemporary readership? And what about yourself: did you grow up in a religiously saturated context?*

I don't think the reader needs to be well versed in the Bible to understand what faith means to different characters. It should be clear enough by context. I trust the reader enough to let them catch up or catch on to things they may not know by giving them enough situational clues. I'm not going to stop what's going on to explain, say, the varying factions in the Jewish resistance to the British Mandate in Palestine. Ideally, the reader feels all of this through the characters' points of view in action rather than being spoon-fed. While I was part of the church as a child, I wouldn't say my background is saturated with religion. I'm Episcopalian, which people here call "Catholic Light." As to the importance of the allusions and references, in many cases these are some of the few moments in which characters pause and imagine something beyond this material world, so they say more about the characters than their daily activities.

8. Many reviewers have been fascinated with the way in which you create American society in terms of a consumer culture-universe in each new novel. Brand names, fast food chains, music, films. Is this a way to create some sort of authenticity or "reality effect" or "Americanness"? On a somewhat related note, I wondered why you chose the Fleetwood Mac references as epigraphs in The Good Wife. *Can you speak to that?*

Using the language and imagery of pop/consumer culture (U.S. or otherwise) has to make sense for the characters. If they're involved in a certain subculture of it, then you need to follow them there and know what the iconography means. Certainly, it means something when the Latvian Holocaust survivor who's risking his life to fight the British relaxes after a mission with a bottle of Johnnie Walker. In contemporary U.S. culture, branding is king (okay, president), and how deeply characters are influenced by or involved in it is an organic way of situating them. Likewise, their relationship to the products of the mass media, whether that's the rap Crest identifies with in *Everyday People* or Arlene's surprise and grief over the death of Cyd Charisse in *Emily, Alone*. Will future readers have any clue what these things mean, like when Leopold Bloom sings advertising ditties to himself in Ulysses? I'm not sure, but, like Joyce, I'm trying to build a world with weight and extension.

I thought that, given the time and place, Patty would naturally be a big fan of that poppier version of Fleetwood Mac, whose "The Chain" was played endlessly on the radio then (and still is!). The lyrics seem to fit her situation perfectly. I'd wanted to quote the whole song, breaking it up between sections, and got permission from four of the band's members, but Stevie Nicks wouldn't give me permission, so I quoted just a few lines under what's termed "fair use."

9. City of Secrets *is a book about terrorism in another time and place. Why did you pick this particular setting?*

Having grown up in the era of bombings and hijackings, I've always been fascinated by the moral choices around the use of political violence. The bombing of the King David Hotel seemed especially interesting in that the hotel, while housing the administrative offices of the British Mandate, wasn't fully a hard target, and the bombers killed dozens of civilians. How did the people involved come to make that choice, and what did it do to them? I wanted to find out in a more honest way than Conrad in *The Secret Agent* and, when I discovered that some of the people involved had been victims of political violence by both the Nazis and the Russians (as well as the British), the questions became even more fraught.

10. Dogs play a special role in the literary O'Nan universe. In Wish You Were Here *the dog, Rufus, is even the narrative focalizer for a short section of the text. A joke? Your own dogs appear in the dedication of the novel.*

Rufus and his relationships with Emily and Henry are an important part of the Maxwell books, and maybe that's because once our children left for college, I spent at least part of my writing days alone with our dogs. I'd always like the dog's point of view section in William Maxwell's *So Long, See You Tomorrow,* and in *Wish You Were Here,* I'd already given point of view sections to everyone else, so I decided Rufus deserved one too. And like William Maxwell, I had to fight my editor to keep it.

11. You have many readers abroad and your work has been translated into many languages. Are you usually in touch with the translators of your work and involved in the process in any way?

I work closely with Thomas Gunkel on the German translations, partly because he's so dedicated. He wants to get everything right and is so thorough that he often finds mistakes of mine that my American editors and copyeditors have missed. For a few of the books, typically ones that involve specific American subcultures, I've worked with my French translators, but most of the other translators go off and do them alone.

12. For a reader who wants to get a first glimpse at you as a writer: is there a book in your oeuvre that you would recommend as a first-contact reading?

Snow Angels is a good introduction to my work. It's both intimate and eventful, nostalgic and hard-edged, does some interesting things formally (I hope), and it's short.

13. Are there characters in your novels that you would specifically consider as alter egos of the author, perhaps in part?

Arthur, Marjorie, Jacob, Crest, Brand, Emily, Henry—they're all me in some way. Fitzgerald said that to write a character he had to find some emotion in them that he could understand, and I think I'm that way too.

14. And one last thing: I noted down that Quentin Tarantino optioned the film rights to The Speed Queen. *True or false? Which of your novels have been secured for film versions? Will there be any projects in the near future that you know of?*

A production company that still does the music for Tarantino's films originally optioned *Speed Queen* twenty years ago. Since then it's gone through a few different companies' hands, including one that had Christina Ricci attached to direct and star in it. Never happened. Right now, several of the novels are under option, including *A Prayer for the Dying, The Odds,* and *Emily, Alone.* You never know, but I'm always hopeful, because David Gordon Green did such a good job with *Snow Angels.*

NOTES

Chapter 1: Understanding Stewart O'Nan

1. "Stewart O'Nan: Our Best Working Novelist," interview with Evison.
2. "Steward O'Nan: Our Best Working Novelist."
3. "The Exchange: Stewart O'Nan," interview with Michaud.
4. Vincent, "Faces in the Crowd."
5. Corrigan, "Joy of the Mundane."
6. James, "Miss Braddon," 110.
7. Mesch, "Mieses Essen."
8. Cf. "Book Prize Preview: Stewart O'Nan," interview with Kellogg.
9. Baldwin, "Everybody's Protest Novel"; and Berlant, *The Female Complaint.*
10. Howells, "Criticism and Fiction," 301.
11. Duncan, "Stewart O'Nan Biography."
12. Hall, "Encoding/Decoding."
13. Benson, review of *Snow Angels.*
14. See, for instance, Van de Ven, review of *Snow Angels.*
15. "Rain Taxi Talks with Stewart O'Nan," interview with *Rain Taxi.*

Chapter 2: Noir-Western and Morality Play

1. Duncan, "Stewart O'Nan Biography."
2. Kipen, "The Town Is Dying Around Him"; and Steinberg and Zaleski. "Forecasts: Fiction."
3. Wald, *Contagious.*
4. Smith, *Virgin Land,* 123–32; and Marx, *Machine in the Garden.*
5. See Waugh and Gallagher, *Wars within a War,* 221.
6. Wald, *Contagious.*
7. Fludernik, "Second Person Fiction," 218.
8. McCarthy, "Story of Everyday Horror."
9. McCarthy, "Story of Everyday Horror."
10. Eder, "Prayer for the Dying."
11. Tompkins, *West of Everything,* 35 and 24.
12. Tompkins, *West of Everything,* 92.
13. Tompkins, *West of Everything,* 37–39.
14. Tompkins, *West of Everything,* 20.
15. Wright, "Curse of O'Nan."

16. Duncan, "Stewart O'Nan Biography."
17. McCarthy, "Time of Plagues."

Chapter 3: Gothic Horror and Everyday Gothic

1. Khapaeva, *Celebration of Death,* 7 and 9.
2. Khapaeva, *Celebration of Death,* 13.
3. Bowen, "Gothic Motifs."
4. Murphy, *Suburban Gothic,* 200.
5. Brite, "Unholy Trinity."
6. "Date with Death," interview with McDonald.
7. "Date with Death."
8. Freeman, "The American Dream."
9. Coleridge, *Biographia Literaria,* 6.
10. Brôcan, "Alltagsmenschen."
11. Kirkus Review of *The Night Country.*
12. Winkels, "Wer weiß schon, was die Toten wollen."
13. Khapaeva, *Celebration of Death,* 13 and 18.
14. McHale, *Postmodernist Fiction.*
15. Brôcan, "Eine Chronik des Schreckens."
16. Charles, "Industry of Hope and Grief."
17. Genette, "Discours du récit."
18. Frisch, *Arlen & Harburg.*
19. Rushdie, in Frisch, *Arlen & Harburg,* 126–27.
20. Charles, "Industry of Hope and Grief."
21. Todorov, "Typology of Detective Fiction," 44.
22. Di Prisco, review of *Songs for the Missing.*
23. Wagner, "Have You Seen My Daughter?"
24. Bowen, "Gothic Motifs."

Chapter 4: Inside/Outside

1. See Davis, *Are Prisons Obsolete?*; and Gilmore, *Golden Gulag.*
2. "A Conversation with Stewart O'Nan," interview with Trucks, 186.
3. "A Conversation with Stewart O'Nan," 188.
4. "A Conversation with Stewart O'Nan," 192.
5. Primeau, *Romance of the Road,* 1.
6. See Orgeron, *Road Movies*; and Roberts, "Western Meets Eastwood."
7. See, for instance, Ganser, *Roads of Her Own.*
8. Corrigan, *Cinema without Walls,* 143.
9. Mayer, "Just Driving," 379.
10. Mayer, "Just Driving," 376.
11. "We're Not Making a Lot of World-Class Ballet," interview with Hogan.
12. Mayer, "Just Driving," 371.
13. Winkels, "White Trash."
14. "A Conversation with Stewart O'Nan," interview with Trucks, 187.
15. "We're Not Making a Lot of World-Class Ballet," interview with Hogan.
16. Brigham, *American Road Narratives,* 4.
17. Primeau, *Romance of the Road,* 1.
18. Anne Stockton, accessed September 18, 2019, www.annestockton.com/about/.

19. Anne Stockton, e-mail message to Alex Sukles, September 8, 2019.

20. O'Nan, quoted by Stockton on her website, accessed January 20, 2020, https://www.annestockton.com/speedqueen/onan.htm.

21. Hoban, "Theater Review."

22. Schweizer, *On Waiting*, 2.

23. Fishman, *Women at the Wall.*

24. Althusser, *On the Reproduction of Capitalism: Ideology and Ideological State Apparatuses*, 236.

25. Foucault, *Discipline and Punish*, 9 and 110.

26. Comfort, "Papa's House," 467.

27. Comfort, "Papa's House," 467.

28. Walcutt, *American Literary Naturalism*, 222.

Chapter 5: Social Realism and the Myth of the Middle Class

1. On neocapitalism, see Bellah et al., *Habits of the Heart*, xxv.

2. Connell, *Precarious Labour*, 4.

3. Rich, "Book Review."

4. Riesman, *The Lonely Crowd.*

5. Reynolds, "Beating Heart."

6. Mesch, "Mieses Essen."

7. Rich, "Book Review."

8. Gregg, "Friday Night Drinks"; see also Crary, *24/7*, 19–22.

9. "The Story of Red Lobster," Red Lobster Hospitality LLC, accessed January 27, 2020, https://www.redlobster.com/our-story/our-heritage.

10. Freeman, Review of *Last Night at the Lobster.*

11. Proctor, "Clock Lobster."

12. Geier, Review of *Last Night at the Lobster.*

13. Anderson, *Imagined Communities.*

14. Rich, "Book Review."

15. "Rain Taxi Talks with Stewart O'Nan," interview with *Rain Taxi*."

16. Illouz, *Consuming the Romantic Utopia*, 95.

17. Williams, *Marxism and Literature.*

18. "Exchange: Stewart O'Nan," interview with Michaud.

19. Cavell, *Pursuits of Happiness.*

20. Shumway, "Screwball Comedies."

21. "Rain Taxi Talks with Stewart O'Nan," interview with *Rain Taxi.*

22. Sennett, "Street and Office," 183.

23. Schram, *Return of Ordinary Capitalism*, 10–11.

24. Berlant, *Cruel Optimism.*

25. Rich, "Book Review."

Chapter 6: Habits of the Heart

1. Tocqueville, *Democracy in America;* and Bellah et al., *Habits of the Heart.*

2. Peterson, "Family," 113.

3. On the bourgeois family, see Raymond Williams in Peterson, "Family," 113.

4. Hochschild, *Managed Heart*, 56.

5. Franklin, "Everyday Terrors."

6. Brokaw, *The Greatest Generation.*

7. Tyson, *Critical Theory Today,* 132.
8. Franklin, "Everyday Terrors."
9. Rakoff, "Stewart O'Nan Tells a Widow's Tale."
10. Corrigan, "Joy of the Mundane."
11. Rakoff, "Stewart O'Nan Tells a Widow's Tale."
12. Corrigan, "Joy of the Mundane."
13. Bourdieu, *Distinctions.*
14. Gans, *Popular Culture.*
15. Gans, *Popular Culture,* 81.
16. Gans, *Popular Culture*, 82–83.
17. Bourdieu, *Distinctions.*
18. Bourdieu, *Distinctions,* 193–94.
19. Veblen, "Conspicuous Consumption."
20. Rakoff, "Stewart O'Nan Tells a Widow's Tale."
21. Watzlawick, *The Situation Is Hopeless.*
22. Rakoff, "Stewart O'Nan Tells a Widow's Tale."
23. Smith, "Stewart O'Nan Returns."
24. *Publisher's Weekly* Review of *Henry, Himself.*
25. Donovan, Review of *Henry, Himself;* and Freedenberg, Review of *Henry, Himself.*
26. Athitakis, Review of *Henry, Himself.*
27. Athitakis, Review of *Henry, Himself.*
28. Gwinn, "Narratives of Struggle."
29. Sandberg, "Master of the Mundane."
30. Seaman, "Henry, Himself."
31. Medina, "Color Blindness."
32. O'Driscoll, "Henry, Himself."
33. Smith, "Stewart O'Nan Returns."
34. Bauman, *Retrotopia.*
35. Athitakis, Review of *Henry, Himself.*

Chapter 7: The Hollywood Novel Revisited

1. Weesner, Review of *West of Sunset.*
2. Brown, *Paradise Lost,* 290.
3. Winters, "West of Sunset by Stewart O'Nan."
4. Winters, "West of Sunset by Stewart O'Nan."
5. Brooker-Bowers, *The Hollywood Novel,* ix.
6. Springer, *Hollywood Fictions,* 3 and 5.
7. Springer, *Hollywood Fictions,* 18.
8. Meyers, *Scott Fitzgerald,* 312.
9. Springer, *Hollywood Fictions,* 18.
10. Brown, *Paradise Lost,* 284.
11. Teetor, "This Book about F. Scott Fitzgerald."
12. Teetor, "This Book about F. Scott Fitzgerald."
13. "Fitzgerald, the Troubled Years," interview with John Wilkens.
14. See Cline, *Zelda Fitzgerald;* Milford, *Zelda: A Biography;* Pike, *Subversive Art of Zelda Fitzgerald;* and Wagner-Martin, *Zelda Sayre Fitzgerald.*
15. James, Review of *West of Sunset.*

16. Graham, *A College of One.*
17. Tanz, "JOURNEYS."

Chapter 8: Other Works

1. Wolff, "Drue Heinz Literature Prize."
2. D'Erasmo, "Here Comes the Neighbourhood."
3. For a nuanced definition of that particularly hybrid genre, see the introduction in James Nagel's study.
4. O'Nan, *Everyday People,* 294.
5. D'Erasmo, "Here Comes the Neighbourhood."
6. Blackwood, "Book Review: Readings."
7. O'Nan, "Afterword" in *Poe: A Screenplay,* 250.
8. Vincent, "Onyx Reviews: *Faithful.*"
9. O'Hagan, "Who Needs Babe Ruth."
10. O'Nan, *Names of the Dead,* 308.
11. O'Nan, *Vietnam Reader,* 5.
12. O'Nan, *Vietnam Reader,* 2.
13. O'Nan, *Vietnam Reader,* 3.
14. O'Nan, *Names of the Dead,* 399.
15. O'Nan [Coltrane, pseud.], *A Good Day to Die,* 44.
16. O'Nan [Coltrane, pseud.], *A Good Day to Die,* 95 and 113.
17. O'Nan, "Thirty Odd Minutes."
18. Parker, "The Artist's Reward," 31.
19. O'Nan [Coltrane, pseud.], *A Good Day to Die,* 93.
20. O'Nan, *Circus Fire,* 58.
21. O'Nan, *Circus Fire,* 363.
22. Green, Review of *The Circus Fire,* 335 and 336.
23. Rich, "Stewart O'Nan *City of Secrets.*"
24. O'Nan, *City of Secrets,* 44.
25. Jason, Review of *City of Secrets.*

BIBLIOGRAPHY

Works by Stewart O'Nan

The Circus Fire. New York: Doubleday, 2000.

City of Secrets. New York: Viking, 2016.

Emily, Alone. New York: Viking, 2011.

Everyday People. New York: Grove, 2001.

"A Face in the Crowd," with Stephen King. New York: Scribner e-book, 2012.

Faithful, with Stephen King. New York: Scribner, 2004.

A Good Day to Die [James Coltrane, pseud.]. New York: Norton, 1999.

The Good Wife. New York: Farrar, Straus & Giroux, 2005.

Henry, Himself. New York: Viking, 2019.

In the Walled City. Pittsburgh: University of Pittsburgh Press, 1993.

Introduction to *The Vietnam Reader: The Definitive Collection of American Fiction and Nonfiction on the War,* edited by Stewart O'Nan, 1–6. New York: Anchor, 1998.

Last Night at the Lobster. New York: Viking, 2007.

"The Lost World of Richard Yates: Why a Great Writer of the Age of Anxiety Disappeared from Print." *Boston Review,* October 1, 1999, bostonreview.net/stewart-onan-the-lost-world-of-richard-yates.

"My Mysteries of Pittsburgh: An Alphabet." *Creative Nonfiction* 15 (Spring 2000): 31–44, www.jstor.org/stable/44362933.

The Names of the Dead. New York: Doubleday, 1996.

The Night Country. New York: Farrar, Straus & Giroux, 2003.

The Odds. New York: Viking, 2012.

Poe: A Screenplay. Illustrated by Jill Bauman. Baltimore: Lonely Roads, 2008.

A Prayer for the Dying. New York: Holt, 1999.

"Scratch the Island from the Map." *Outside Magazine,* November 1998; and *Outside Online,* May 2, 2004, https://www.outsideonline.com/1886361/scratch-island-map.

Snow Angels. New York: Doubleday, 1994.

Songs for the Missing. New York: Viking, 2008.

The Speed Queen. New York: Doubleday, 1997.

West of Sunset. New York: Viking, 2015.

Wish You Were Here. New York: Grove, 2002.

A World Away. New York: Holt, 1998.

The Vietnam Reader: The Definitive Collection of American Fiction and Nonfiction on the War, edited by Stewart O'Nan. New York: Anchor, 1998.

Interviews with Stewart O'Nan

"Book Prize Preview: Stewart O'Nan." Interview by Carolyn Kellogg from *Hot Metal Bridge. Los Angeles Times Blogs,* April 4, 2008, latimesblogs.latimes.com/jacketcopy/2008/04/book-prize-prev.html.

"A Conversation with Stewart O'Nan." Interview by Rob Trucks. *The Pleasure of Influence. Conversation with American Male Fiction Writers,* edited by Rob Trucks, 175–203. West Lafayette: Purdue University Press, 2002.

"A Date with Death." Interview by Jay McDonald. *BookPage,* October 2003, bookpage.com/interviews/8218-stewart-onan-fiction#.XWzlm_ZuLct.

"The Exchange: Stewart O'Nan." Interview by Jon Michaud. *New Yorker,* January 13, 2012, www.newyorker.com/books/page-turner/the-exchange-stewart-onan.

"Fitzgerald, the Troubled Years." Interview by John Wilkens. *San Diego Union Tribune,* January 26, 2015, www.sandiegouniontribune.com/entertainment/books/sdut-stewart-onan-scott-fitzgerald-interview-2015jan26-htmlstory.html.

"Rain Taxi Talks with Stewart O'Nan." Interview by *Rain Taxi,* February 1, 2012, www.raintaxi.com/rain-taxi-talks-with-stewart-onan/.

"Stewart O'Nan: Our Best Working Novelist?" Interview by Jonathan Evison. *Salon,* February 29, 2012, www.salon.com/2012/02/29/stewart_onan_our_best_working_novelist/.

"Thirty Odd Minutes with Stewart O'Nan." Interview by Eric Sandberg. *KNOCK AND KNOWALL,* April 5, 2019, www.knockandknowall.com/articles/30-odd-minutes-with-stewart-onan.

"We're Not Making a Lot of World-Class Ballet Here, Okay?" Interview by Ron Hogan. *Beatrice.* 1997, accessed July 31, 2019, www.beatrice.com/interviews/onan/.

Secondary Sources

Althusser, Louis. *On the Reproduction of Capitalism: Ideology and Ideological State Apparatuses.* London: Verso, 2014.

Anderson, Benedict. *Imagined Communities: Reflections on the Origin and Spread of Nationalism.* London: Verso, 1983.

Athitakis, Mark. Review of *Henry, Himself,* by Stewart O'Nan. *Star Tribune,* April 5, 2019. www.startribune.com/review-henry-himself-by-stewart-o-nan/508127492/.

Baldwin, James. "Everybody's Protest Novel." In *Notes of a Native Son,* by James Baldwin, 9–17. Boston: Beacon, 1955.

Bauman, Zygmunt. *Retrotopia.* Cambridge: Polity, 2017.

Bellah, Robert N., Richard Madsen, William M. Sullivan, Ann Swidler, and Steven M. Tipton, eds. *Habits of the Heart: Individualism and Commitment in American Life. With a New Preface.* Berkeley: University of California Press, 1996.

Benson, Robert. Review of *Snow Angels,* by Stewart O'Nan. *The Sewanee Review* 104, no. 3 (Summer 1996): lix–lxii.

Berlant, Lauren. *Cruel Optimism.* Durham, N.C.: Duke University Press, 2011.

———. *The Female Complaint.* Durham, N.C.: Duke University Press, 2008.

Blackwood, Scott. "Book Review: Readings. Stewart O'Nan." Review of *Everyday People,* by Stewart O'Nan. *Austin Chronicle,* March 9, 2001, www.austinchronicle.com/books/2001-03-09/everyday-people-a-novel/.

Bourdieu, Pierre. *Distinctions: A Social Critique of the Judgement of Taste.* Translated by Richard Nice. Cambridge, Mass.: Harvard University Press, 1984.

Bowen, John. "Gothic Motifs." *British Library*, May 15, 2014, http://www.bl.uk/romantics-and-victorians/articles/gothic-motifs.

Brigham, Ann. *American Road Narratives: Reimagining Mobility in Literature and Film*. Charlottesville: University of Virginia Press, 2015.

Brite, Poppy Z. "Unholy Trinity." Review of *The Night Country*, by Stewart O'Nan. *The Guardian*, October 30, 2004, www.theguardian.com/books/2004/oct/30/features reviews.guardianreview25.

Brôcan, Jürgen. "Alltagsmenschen, Alltagshorror: Die Romankonzepte des Erzählers Stewart O'Nan." *Neue Züricher Zeitung*, October 16, 2004, p. 65.

———. "Eine Chronik des Schreckens." Review of *Alle, alle lieben dich* (German edition of *Songs for the Missing*), by Stewart O'Nan. Neue Züricher Zeitung, March 18, 2004, www.nzz.ch/eine_chronik_des_schreckens-1.2216344.

Brokaw, Tom. *The Greatest Generation*. New York: Random House, 1998.

Brooker-Bowers, Nancy. *The Hollywood Novel and Other Novels about Film, 1912–1982: An Annotated Bibliography*. New York: Garland, 1985.

Brown, David S. *Paradise Lost: A Life of F. Scott Fitzgerald*. Cambridge, Mass.: Belknap Press of Harvard University Press, 2017.

Cavell, Stanley. *Pursuits of Happiness: The Hollywood Comedy of Remarriage*. Cambridge, Mass.: Harvard University Press, 1981.

Charles, Ron. "The Industry of Hope and Grief." Review of *Songs for the Missing*, by Stewart O'Nan. *Washington Post*, November 23, 2008, www.washingtonpost.com/wp-dyn/content/article/2008/11/20/AR2008112002788.html.

Cline, Sally. *Zelda Fitzgerald: Her Voice in Paradise*. New York: Arcade, 2003.

Coleridge, Samuel Taylor. *Biographia Literaria*. Vol. 2. Edited by J. Shawcross. Oxford: Clarendon Press, 1907. Originally published in 1817.

Comfort, Megan L. "'Papa's House': The Prison as Domestic and Social Satellite." *Ethnography* 3, no. 4 (December 2002): 467–99, doi:10.1177/1466138102003004017.

Connell, Liam. *Precarious Labour and the Contemporary Novel*. Cham: Springer, 2017.

Corrigan, Maureen. "The Joy of the Mundane in 'Emily, Alone'." Review of *Emily, Alone*, by Stewart O'Nan. *National Public Radio Book Reviews*, March 22, 2011, www.npr.org/2011/03/29/134762678/the-joy-of-the-mundane-in-emily-alone.

Corrigan, Timothy. *A Cinema without Walls: Movies and Culture after Vietnam*. New Brunswick, N.J.: Rutgers University Press, 1991.

Crary, Jonathan. *24/7: Late Capitalism and the Ends of Sleep*. London: Verso, 2013.

Davis, Angela Y. *Are Prisons Obsolete?* New York: Seven Stories, 2003.

D'Erasmo, Stacey. "Here Comes the Neighborhood." Review of *Everyday People*, by Stewart O'Nan. *New York Times*, February 25, 2001, movies2.nytimes.com/books/01/02/25/reviews/010225.25derast.html.

Di Prisco, Joseph. Review of *Songs for the Missing*, by Stewart O'Nan. *San Francisco Chronicle*, November 16, 2008, www.sfgate.com/books/article/Songs-for-the-Missing-by-Stewart-O-Nan-3185236.php.

Donovan, Deborah. Review of *Henry, Himself*, by Stewart O'Nan. *Book Page*, April 2019. bookpage.com/reviews/23848-stewart-onan-henry-himself-fiction.

Duncan, Andy. "Stewart O'Nan Biography." N.d., accessed July 31, 2019. biography.jrank.org/pages/4644/O-nan-Stewart.html.

Eder, Richard. "'A Prayer for the Dying': A Godly Man Called Jacob, in a Plague's Crucible." Review of *A Prayer for the Dying*, by Stewart O'Nan. *New York Times*, April 12, 1999, archive.nytimes.com/www.nytimes.com/library/books/041299onan-book-review.html.

Ehrenreich, Barbara. *Nickel and Dimed: On (Not) Getting by in America.* New York: Holt, 2001.

Fishman, Laura T. *Women at the Wall: A Study of Prisoners' Wives Doing Time on the Outside.* Albany: State University of New York Press, 1990.

Fitzgerald, Scott. "The Crack-Up: A Desolately Frank Document from One for Whom the Salt of Life Has Lost Its Savor." *Esquire,* February 1, 1936, classic.esquire.com/article/1936/2/1/the-crack-up.

———. "Handle with Care: Vivisection of a Hardening Soul by One Who Had No Use for Anaesthesia on Himself." *Esquire,* April 1, 1936, classic.esquire.com/article/1936/4/1/handle-with-care.

———. "Pasting It Together: Shoring Up the Fragments against the Ruin Left in the Wake of That Psycho-Physical Storm: A Crack-Up." *Esquire,* March 1, 1936, classic.esquire.com/article/1936/3/1/pasting-it-together.

Fludernik, Monika. "Second Person Fiction: Narrative You as Addressee and/or Protagonist." *Arbeiten aus Anglistik und Amerikanistik* 18, no. 2 (1993): 217–47.

Foucault, Michel. *Discipline and Punish: The Birth of the Prison.* Translated by Alan Sheridan. New York: Vintage, 1995.

Franklin, Ruth. "Everyday Terrors." Review of *Wish You Were Here,* by Stewart O'Nan. *New York Times,* May 26, 2002, www.nytimes.com/2002/05/26/books/everyday-terrors.html.

Freedenberg, Harvey. Review of *Henry, Himself,* by Stewart O'Nan. *Bookreporter,* April 19, 2019, https://www.bookreporter.com/reviews/henry-himself.

Freeman, John. Review of *Last Night at the Lobster,* by Stewart O'Nan. *BarnesandNoble Review.com,* November 5, 2007, www.barnesandnoble.com/review/last-night-at-the-lobster.

———. "The American Dream Turns to Nightmare." Review of *The Night Country,* by Stewart O'Nan. *Independent,* October 29, 2004, www.independent.co.uk/arts-entertainment/books/reviews/the-night-country-by-stewart-onan-755063.html.

Frisch, Walter. *Arlen & Harburg's* Over the Rainbow. Oxford: Oxford University Press, 2017.

Gans, Herbert J. *Popular Culture and High Culture: An Analysis and Evaluation of Taste.* New York: Basic Books, 1974.

Ganser, Alexandra. *Roads of Her Own: "Gendered Space and Mobility in American Women's Road Narratives, 1970–2000."* Amsterdam: Rodopi, 2009.

Geier, Thom. Review of *Last Night at the Lobster,* by Stewart O'Nan. *Entertainment Weekly,* November 2, 2007, ew.com/article/2007/11/02/last-night-lobster/.

Genette, Gérard. "Discours du récit." In *Figures III.* Paris: Seuil, 1972, 67–282.

Gilmore, Ruth Wilson. *Golden Gulag: Prisons, Surplus, Crisis, and Opposition in Globalizing California.* Berkeley: University of California Press, 2007.

Graham, Sheilah. *A College of One: The Story of How F. Scott Fitzgerald Educated the Woman He Loved.* New York: Viking, 1967.

Green, Harvey. Review of *The Circus Fire: A True Story,* by Stewart O'Nan. *New England Quarterly* 74, no. 2 (June 2001): 335–37, www.jstor.org/stable/3185487.

Gregg, Melissa. "On Friday Night Drinks: Workplace Affects in the Age of the Cubicle." In *The Affect Theory Reader,* edited by Melissa Gregg, and Gregory J. Seigworth, 250–68. Durham, N.C.: Duke University Press, 2010.

Gwinn, Mary Ann. "Narratives of Struggle, from Political Strife in Vichy France to a Man

Confronting Death." Review of *The Flight Portfolio*, by Julie Orringer, and *Henry, Himself*, by Stewart O'Nan. *Seattle Times*, June 1, 2019, www.yakimaherald.com/narratives-of-struggle-from-political-strife-in-vichy-france-to/article_ed62ad6b-d194-5bb1-bb54-f761bd1f566c.html.

Hall, Stuart. "Encoding/Decoding." In *Culture, Media, Language: Working Papers in Cultural Studies, 1972–79*, edited by Stuart Hall, Dorothy Hobson, Andrew Lowe, and Paul Willis, 128–38. London: Routledge, 1992.

Hemingway, Ernest. "The Snows of Kilimanjaro." *Esquire*, August 1, 1936, classic.esquire.com/article/1936/8/1/the-snows-of-kilimanjaro.

Hoban, Phoebe. "Theater Review: A Death-Row Tale That Turns Ho-Hum." *New York Times*, November 5, 2006. archive.nytimes.com/query.nytimes.com/gst/fullpage-9C01E4D7133FF936A35752C1A9609C8B63.html?pagewanted=print.

Hochschild, Arlie R. *The Managed Heart: Commercialization of Human Feeling*. Berkeley: University of California Press, 1983.

Howells, William Dean. "Criticism and Fiction." Reprinted in *Selected Literary Criticism*. Vol. 2, *1886–97*. Bloomington: Indiana University Press, 1993.

Illouz, Eva. *Consuming the Romantic Utopia: Love and the Cultural Contradictions of Capitalism*. Berkeley: University of California Press, 1997.

James, Caryn. Review of *West of Sunset*, by Stewart O'Nan. *New York Times*, February 20, 2015, www.nytimes.com/2015/02/22/books/review/west-of-sunset-by-stewart-onan.html.

James, Henry. "Miss Braddon." In *Notes and Reviews*, 108–16. Cambridge, Mass.: Dunster House, 1921.

Jason, Philip K. Review of *City of Secrets*, by Stewart O'Nan. *Jewish Book Council*, July 5, 2016, www.jewishbookcouncil.org/book/city-of-secrets.

Khapaeva, Dina. *The Celebration of Death in Contemporary Culture*. Ann Arbor: University of Michigan Press, 2017.

Kipen, David. "The Town Is Dying around Him / O'Nan's 'Prayer' Looks at Mortality, Morality." Review of *A Prayer for the Dying*, by Stewart O'Nan. *SFGate*, April 22, 1999, www.sfgate.com/books/article/The-Town-Is-Dying-Around-Him-O-Nan-s-Prayer-2934917.php.

Kirkus Review of *The Night Country*, by Stewart O'Nan. *Kirkus Review*, May 20, 2010, www.kirkusreviews.com/book-reviews/stewart-onan/the-night-country/.

Lesy, Michael. *Wisconsin Death Trip*. New York: Pantheon, 1973.

Marx, Leo. *The Machine in the Garden: Technology and the Pastoral Ideal in America*. Oxford: Oxford University Press.

Mayer, Ruth. "'Just Driving': Contemporary Road Novels and the Triviality of the Outlaw Existence." In *Space in America: Theory, History, Culture*, edited by Klaus Benesch and Kerstin Schmidt, 369–84. Amsterdam: Rodopi, 2005.

McCarthy, Peter. "In a Time of Plagues." Review of *A Prayer for the Dying*, by Stewart O'Nan. *Washington Post*, May 16, 1999, www.washingtonpost.com/archive/entertainment/books/1999/05/16/in-a-time-of-plagues/cad998f1-4f9c-4a8f-94d2-c6f4437cdf76/?tid=ss_tw.

McCarthy, Tim. "A Story of Everyday Horror that's Stubbornly Religious." Review of *A Prayer for the Dying*, by Stewart O'Nan. *National Catholic Reporter Online*, May 7, 1999, natcath.org/NCR_Online/archives2/1999b/050799/050799n.htm.

McHale, Brian. *Postmodernist Fiction*. London: Routledge, 1987.

Medina, José. "Color Blindness, Meta-Ignorance, and the Racial Imagination." In *Critical Philosophy of Race* 1, no. 1, Special Issue: *Critical Philosophy of Race beyond the Black/White Binary* (2013): 38–67.

Mesch, Stefan. "Mieses Essen, McJobs, halbverdaute Gefühle. In 'Letzte Nacht' begleitet Stewart O'Nan einen Helden des Alltags an der US-Ostküste." Review of *Letzte Nacht* (German edition of *Last Night at the Lobster*), by Stewart O'Nan. *literaturkritik .de,* May 2008, literaturkritik.de/id/11884.

Meyers, Jeffrey. *Scott Fitzgerald: A Biography.* New York: Harper Collins, 1994.

Milford, Nancy. *Zelda: A Biography.* New York: Harper & Row, 1970.

Morrison, Toni. *Playing in the Dark: Whiteness and the Literary Imagination.* Cambridge, Mass.: Harvard University Press, 1992.

Murphy, Bernice M. *The Suburban Gothic in American Popular Culture.* Basingstoke, U.K.: Palgrave MacMillan, 2009.

Nagel, James. *The Contemporary American Short-Story Cycle: The Ethnic Resonance of Genre.* Baton Rouge: Louisiana State University Press, 2001.

O'Driscoll, Bill. "'Henry, Himself': An Enduring Tribute to an Ordinary Life." Review of *Henry, Himself,* by Stewart O'Nan. *Pittsburgh Post-Gazette,* April 9, 2019, www.post-gazette.com/ae/books/2019/04/09/Stewart-O-Nan-Henry-Himself/stories/201904090006.

O'Hagan, Sean. "Who Needs Babe Ruth?" Review of *Faithful,* by Stewart O'Nan and Stephen King. *Guardian,* January 16, 2005, www.theguardian.com/books/2005/jan/16/stephenking.sportandleisure.

Orgeron, Devin. *Road Movies: From Muybridge and Méliès to Lynch and Kiarostami.* Basingstoke, U.K.: Palgrave Macmillan, 2008.

Parker, Dorothy. "The Artist's Reward." *New Yorker*, November 30, 1929, 28–31.

Peterson, Carla L. "Family." In *Keywords for American Cultural Studies,* edited by Bruce Burgett, and Glenn Hendler, 112–16. New York: New York University Press, 2007.

Pike, Deborah. *The Subversive Art of Zelda Fitzgerald.* Columbia: University of Missouri Press, 2017.

Primeau, Ronald. *Romance of the Road: The Literature of the American Highway.* Bowling Green, Ohio: Bowling Green State University Popular Press, 1996.

Proctor, Minna. "Clock Lobster." Review of *Last Night at the Lobster,* by Stewart O'Nan. *Bookforum,* December/January 2008, www.bookforum.com/print/1404/stewart-o-nan-s-last-night-at-the-lobster-1395.

Publisher's Weekly, Review of *Henry, Himself* by Stewart O'Nan. *Publishers Weekly,* May 15, 2019, www.publishersweekly.com/978-0-7352-2304-2.

Rakoff, Joanna Smith. "Stewart O'Nan Tells a Widow's Tale." Review of *Emily, Alone,* by Stewart O'Nan. *New York Times,* April 1, 2011, www.nytimes.com/2011/04/03/books/review/book-review-emily-alone-by-stewart-onan.html.

Reynolds, Susan Salters. "The Beating Heart of a Lifeless Town." Review of *Last Night at the Lobster,* by Stewart O'Nan. *Los Angeles Times,* November 5, 2007, www.latimes.com/archives/la-xpm-2007-nov-05-et-book5-story.html.

Rich, Nathaniel. "Book Review: Last Night at the Lobster." Review of *Last Night at the Lobster* by Stewart O'Nan. *New York Times,* November 5, 2007, www.nytimes.com/2007/12/04/arts/04iht-lobsterreview.8584427.html.

———. "Stewart O'Nan *City of Secrets* Review and Interview." *Narrative Species* (blog), May 16, 2016, narrativespecies.wordpress.com/2016/05/16/stewart-onan-city-of-secrets-review-and-interview/.

Riesman, David. *The Lonely Crowd: A Study of the Changing American Character.* With Nathan Glazer and Reuel Denney. Abridged edition with a 1969 preface. New Haven, Conn.: Yale University Press, 1989.

Roberts, Shari "Western Meets Eastwood: Genre and Gender on the Road." In *The Road Movie Book,* edited by Ina Rae Hark, and Steven Cohan, 45–69. London: Routledge, 1997.

Sandberg, Eric. "Master of the Mundane: Stewart O'Nan—Henry, Himself." Review. *KNOCKANDKNOWALL* (blog), March 17, 2019, www.knockandknowall.com/articles/book-review-stewart-onan-henry-himself.

Schram, Sanford F. *The Return of Ordinary Capitalism: Neoliberalism, Precarity, Occupy.* Oxford: Oxford University Press, 2015.

Schweizer, Harold. *On Waiting.* Oxon: Routledge, 2008.

Seaman, Donna. "*Henry, Himself.* O'Nan, Stewart (Author)." Review. *Booklist Online,* April 1, 2019, www.booklistonline.com/Henry-Himself/pid=9717879.

Sennett, R. "Street and Office: Two Sources of Identity." In *On the Edge: Living with Global Capitalism,* edited by Will Hutton, and Anthony Giddens, 175–90. London: Vintage, 2001.

Shumway, David R. "Screwball Comedies: Constructing Romance, Mystifying Marriage." *Cinema Journal* 30, no. 4 (Summer 1991): 7–23.

Slotkin, Richard. *Regeneration through Violence: The Mythology of the American Frontier, 1600–1860.* Norman: University of Oklahoma Press, 1973.

Smith, Dominic. "Stewart O'Nan Returns to the Fictional Maxwell Family." Review of *Henry, Himself,* by Stewart O'Nan. *New York Times,* May 2, 2019, www.nytimes.com/2019/05/02/books/review/stewart-onan-henry-himself.html.

Smith, Henry Nash. *Virgin Land: The West as Symbol and Myth.* Cambridge, Mass.: Harvard University Press, 1950.

Springer, John Parris. *Hollywood Fictions: The Dream Factory in American Popular Literature.* Norman: University of Oklahoma Press, 2000.

Steinberg, Sybil, and Jeff Zaleski. "Forecasts: Fiction." Review of *A Prayer for the Dying,* by Stewart O'Nan. *Publishers Weekly* 246, no. 2 (January 11, 1999): 52.

Tanz, Jason. "JOURNEYS; Lost Weekend: F. Scott and Budd Go to Dartmouth." *New York Times* February 7, 2003, www.nytimes.com/2003/02/07/travel/journeys-lost-weekend-f-scott-and-budd-go-to-dartmouth.html.

Teetor, Paul. "This Book about F. Scott Fitzgerald in L.A. Is the Best Hollywood Novel in Years." Review of *West of Sunset,* by Stewart O'Nan. *LA Weekly,* January 27, 2015, www.laweekly.com/arts/this-book-about-f-scott-fitzgerald-in-la-is-the-best-hollywood-novel-in-years-5352167.

Tocqueville, Alexis de. *Democracy in America.* 2 vols. Edited by Daniel Boorstein. New York: Vintage, 1990.

Todorov, Tzvetan. "The Typology of Detective Fiction." In *The Poetics of Prose,* 42–52. Oxford: Blackwell, 1977.

Tompkins, Jane. *West of Everything: The Inner Life of Westerns.* Oxford: Oxford University Press, 1992.

Tyson, Lois. *Critical Theory Today: A User-Friendly Guide.* 2nd ed. New York: Routledge, 2012.

Van de Ven, Lisa. Review of *Snow Angels* by Stewart O'Nan. *Popmatters,* April 16, 2008, www.popmatters.com/snow-angels-by-stewart-onan-2496159859.html.

Veblen, Thorstein. "Conspicuous Consumption." In *Theory of the Leisure Class: An Economic Study of Institutions,* 68–101. New York: MacMillan, 1912.

Vincent, Beth. "Faces in the Crowd." Review of *A Face in the Crowd,* by Stephen King and Stewart O'Nan. *bevvincent.com,* August 23, 2012, www.bevvincent.com/non-fiction/fearnet/faces-in-the-crowd/.

———. "Onyx Reviews: *Faithful* by Stewart O'Nan and Stephen King." *bevvinvent.com,* n.d., accessed September 18, 2019, www.bevvincent.com/onyx/onan-faithful.html.

Wagner, Erica. "Have You Seen My Daughter?" Review of *Songs for the Missing,* by Stewart O'Nan. *New York Times,* December 19, 2008, www.nytimes.com/2008/12/21/books/review/Wagner-t.html.

Wagner-Martin, Linda. *Zelda Sayre Fitzgerald: An American Woman's Life.* Basingstoke, U.K.: Palgrave, 2004.

Walcutt, Charles Child. *American Literary Naturalism: A Divided Stream.* Minneapolis: University of Minnesota Press, 1956.

Wald, Priscilla. *Contagious: Cultures, Carriers, and the Outbreak Narrative.* Durham, N.C.: Duke University Press, 2008.

Walton, Emily. *Der Sommer, in dem F. Scott Fitzgerald beinahe einen Kellner zersägte.* Wien: Braumüller, 2016.

Watzlawick, Paul. *The Situation Is Hopeless, But Not Serious: The Pursuit of Unhappiness.* New York: Norton, 1983.

Waugh, Joan, and Gary W. Gallagher, eds. *Wars within a War: Controversy and Conflict over the American Civil War.* Chapel Hill: University of North Carolina Press, 2009.

Weesner, Ted. Review of *West of Sunset,* by Stewart O'Nan. *Boston Globe,* January 17, 2015, www.bostonglobe.com/arts/books/2015/01/17/review-west-sunset-stewart-nan/8QzMZBCZAnT6EPfVVSl4LK/story.html.

Williams, Raymond. *Marxism and Literature.* Oxford: Oxford University Press, 1977.

Winkels, Hubert. "Wer weiß schon, was die Toten wollen." Review of *Halloween* (German edition of *The Night Country*), by Stewart O'Nan. *DIE ZEIT* 5, January 22, 2004, www.zeit.de/2004/05/L-ONan?wt_zmc=sm.ext.zonaudev.mail.ref.zeitde.share.link.x.

———. "White Trash." Review of *Die Speed Queen* (German edition of *The Speed Queen*), by Stewart O'Nan. *DIE ZEIT* 19, April 29, 1998, www.zeit.de/1998/19/White_Trash.

Winters, David. "West of Sunset by Stewart O'Nan: A Fine Fictional F Scott Fitzgerald." Review. *Guardian,* September 3, 2015, www.theguardian.com/books/2015/sep/03/west-of-sunset-by-stewart-onan-review-f-scott-fitzgerald.

Wolff, Tobias. "From the Citation for the 1993 Drue Heinz Literature Prize." In *Grove Atlantic,* n.d., accessed September 18, 2019, https://groveatlantic.com/book/in-the-walled-city/.

Wright, Chris. "The Curse of O'Nan." Review of *A Prayer for the Dying,* by Stewart O'Nan. *Weekly Wire/Boston Phoenix,* May 10, 1999, weeklywire.com/ww/05-10-99/boston_books_1.html.

INDEX